CONTENTS

Acknowledgements		2
Glossary and abbreviations		2
1	An Unholy bloodbath	3
2	Battles in the Marshes	18
3	The Slough of Despond	36
4	The Thriving Armourers	54
5	The Brilliant Blow	63
Bibliography		84
Notes		85

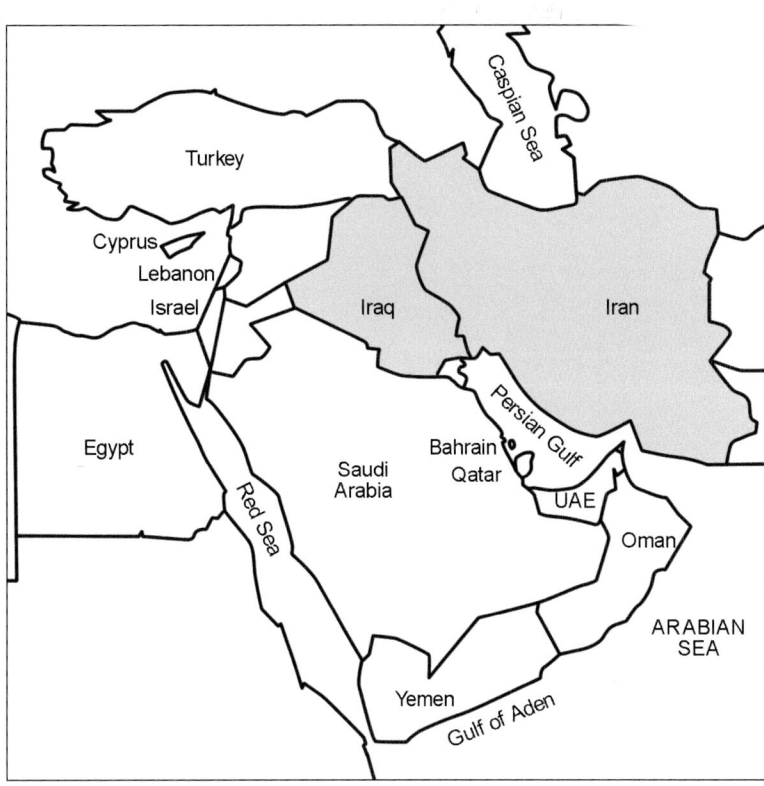

Helion & Company Limited
Unit 8 Amherst Business Centre, Budbrooke Road, Warwick CV34 5WE, England
Tel. 01926 499 619
Email: info@helion.co.uk
Website: www.helion.co.uk
Twitter: @helionbooks
Visit our blog http://blog.helion.co.uk/

Original edition published by Helion & Company 2016. This revised edition published by Helion & Company 2019

Text © E.R. Hooton, Tom Cooper and Farzad Bishop 2016–2019
Colour profiles © Radek Panchartek and Tom Cooper
Maps © George Anderson 2016
Photographs © as individually credited
Printed via Jellyfish Solutions (www.jellyfishsolutions.co.uk)

Designed & typeset by Farr out Publications, Wokingham, Berkshire
Cover design by Paul Hewitt, Battlefield Design (www.battlefield-design.co.uk)

Every reasonable effort has been made to trace copyright holders and to obtain their permission for the use of copyright material. The author and publisher apologize for any errors or omissions in this work, and would be grateful if notified of any corrections that should be incorporated in future reprints or editions of this book.

ISBN 978-1-913118-53-2

British Library Cataloguing-in-Publication Data
A catalogue record for this book is available from the British Library

All rights reserved. No part of this publication may be reproduced, stored in a retrieval system, or transmitted, in any form, or by any means, electronic, mechanical, photocopying, recording or otherwise, without the express written consent of Helion & Company Limited.

We always welcome receiving book proposals from prospective authors.

Acknowledgements

I would like to thank Dr Kevin W. Woods, one of the leading researchers in the Iran-Iraq War, for his extremely useful advice in following certain lines of research and Major General Aladdin Hussein Makki Khamas for his great kindness not only for taking time to respond to my queries from his encyclopaedic knowledge of the Iraqi Army and the war with Iran but also volunteering extra relevant information. He has done so with astonishing speed and with great courtesy both of which I greatly appreciate.

Colonel Pesach Malovany, one of the leading non-Arab authorities on the Iraqi Army, for his assistance and advice. His comprehensive Hebrew-language history of the Iraqi Army *Milhamot Bavel ha-Hadasha,* has been expanded and published in the English language and is one of the best foreign studies of this important army.

Finally my thanks also extend to my fellow writers Tom Cooper and Farzad Bishop whose expertise on the Iran-Iraq War long predates my research into the subject. They have been a vital source of valuable information and corrected my most glaring errors despite their busy professional lives.

Glossary and abbreviations

AFV	Armoured Fighting Vehicle
AK/AKM	Russian for Automat Kalashnikova (general designation for a class of Soviet or former Eastern Bloc-manufactured class of assault rifles)
APC	armoured personnel carrier
ASCC	Air Standardisation Coordinating Committee
ATGM	anti-tank guided missile
CAS	close air support
CIA	Central Intelligence Agency (USA)
COIN	counter-insurgency
COMINT	communications intelligence
ECM	electronic countermeasures
ESM	electronic support measures
ELINT	electronic intelligence
FAC	forward air controller
FEBA	forward edge of battle area
GCC	Gulf Cooperation Council
GMID	General Military Intelligence Directorate (Iraq)
HE	high explosive
IFF	identification friend or foe
IFV	infantry fighting vehicle
IrAAC	Iraqi Army Aviation Corps
IrAF	Iraqi Air Force
IRI	Islamic Republic of Iran
IRIA	Islamic Republic of Iran Army
IRIAA	Islamic Republic of Iran Army Aviation
IRIAF	Islamic Republic of Iran Air Force
IRIN	Islamic Republic of Iran Navy
MANPADS	man-portable air defence system
MBT	main battle tank
MHz	Megahertz, millions of cycles per second
MLR	main line of resistance
MRLS	multiple rocket launch system
NATO	North Atlantic Treaty Organisation
OPEC	Organization of the Petroleum Exporting Countries
ORBAT	Order of Battle
RCC	Revolutionary Command Council (Iraq)
RPG	rocket propelled grenade
SFOH	Southern Front Operations Headquarters (Iraq)
SEAL	Sea, Air, Land (Naval Commandos)
SIGINT	signals intelligence
TAOR	Tactical Area of Responsibility
TOW	Tube-launched, Optically-tracked, Wire-guided ATGM, officially designated BGM-71

1
AN UNHOLY BLOODBATH

By the summer of 1982 Saddam Hussein's regime had seen a tremendous change in fortunes barely 18 months after invading Iran.

In September 1980 Saddam Hussein at-Takriti (usually known as Saddam) tried to exploit the post-Revolution chaos in Iran both to strengthen Iraq's frontiers and to gain control of the Shatt al-Arab, the waterway leading to the great port of Basra (also Basrah). His objective was to seize a long strip of Iranian territory along the frontier, together with a major bridgehead in Khuzestan, to encourage a revolt against the theocratic government of Ayatollah Ruhollah al-Musavi al-Khomeini (Ayatollah Khomeini). Saddam hoped a new government would be more amenable to a diplomatic solution which would give Baghdad control of both disputed border territory and the Shatt al-Arab.

But poor planning, and the absence of any strategic military goals, left the Iraqi Army impaled on the frontier by the end of 1980. Far from encouraging Khomeini's enemies, the invasion helped the clerics to consolidate their power until in 1982 they inflicted two major defeats upon the Iraqi Army – which had to abandon most of the conquered territory, apart from a few toeholds in the extreme north-west of Khuzestan and to the north. With the Israeli invasion of Lebanon in the summer of 1982, Saddam offered Tehran a cease-fire, nominally so they could both fight the Israelis, but the Iranians rejected the offer.

With the expulsion of the invader, Iran's Supreme Defence Council (SDC) considered the next move. The ultimate arbiter of Iranian strategy was Khomeini, who wished to rein-in his troops on the Iranian side of the frontier and consolidate the revolution. Strategy may be driven by passion rather than reason, especially with revolutionary regimes, and the twin desires for revenge and the expansion of God's kingdom on earth were too heady a mixture for the mullahs to resist.[1]

The idea of quitting while ahead was supported by many of the senior members of government, notably President Ali Hosseini Khamenei (Khameneh), Premier Seyyed Mir-Hossein Mousavi and even hard-line Foreign Minister Ali Akbar Velayati. They argued that Iran would be regarded as an aggressor if it crossed the frontier and lose its few Arab friends, including Saudi Arabia which had indicated a willingness to fund Iraqi war reparations to help restore the war-wrecked economy.

They also emphasised that Iran lacked the resources to pursue an offensive strategy at a time when the army faced a major insurgency problem in Kordistan. The Islamic Republic of Iran Army (IRIA) Commander-in-Chief, Brigadier General Qasem Ali Zahirnejhad, echoed the latter concern and noted the armed forces' lack of experience in projecting power when there was a shortage of firepower, mobility and air support, together with significant logistical problems. Compared to Iraq's 3,000 MBTs and 1,800 guns, Iran had only 900 of each, and many of these were unserviceable due to the growing spares shortage. For Zahirnejhad this was a U-turn, for he would later claim that soon after his appointment in 1981, Khomeini had vetoed his plan to drive into Iraq once Abadan had been relieved.

Yet the generals were undermined by the deeply devout and optimistic Commander of the IRIA Ground Forces, Major General Ali Sayad Shirazi, who felt like, Mohsen Rezai, leader of the Islamic Army of the Guardians of the Islamic Revolution (Sepah-e Pasdaran-e Enghelab-e Eslami) – or Pasdaran – that the enemy was on the point of collapse and that the zeal of Islam's devoted soldiers would overcome all obstacles. They were joined by the Parliament's highly influential Speaker, and 'voice' of the Iranian parliament, Akbar Hashemi-Rafsanjani, to persuade Khomeini to sanction a cross-border offensive.

Shirazi stated: "We will continue the war until Saddam Hussein is overthrown so that we can pray at Karbala and Jerusalem", while Rafsanjani claimed: "We are not going to attack any territory. We only want our rights (including the overthrow of Saddam)." They argued that the massed Iraqi Army on the frontier could strike again, indeed artillery bombardments upon of Khorammshahr and Abadan were already taking Iranian lives. These could be shielded only by establishing a buffer zone in enemy territory which would be a valuable bargaining chip to force Saddam to the negotiating table. With unconscious irony, Tehran's radicals were echoing almost the same arguments which Saddam had made in justifying his invasion two years earlier. The radicals also feared that the end of the war

Operation Beit-ol-Moqaddas resulted in the destruction of one Iraqi division and the mauling of several others, and up to 200 Iraqi tanks – including these five T-55s – being captured by the Iranians. Thus began a new phase of the Iran-Iraq War, during which Tehran staged ever bigger offensives. (Tom Cooper Collection)

Iraqi prisoners of war stream out of Khorramshahr after one of the defeats of early 1982. Between 12,000 and 13,000 Iraqi troops were captured – of whom the Iranians summarily executed about 2,000 – forcing Baghdad to rebuild a number of battered divisions. Many of the captured Iraqis were Shi'a, and some of them were eventually persuaded by the Iranians to change sides. (Tom Cooper Collection)

would destroy a national unifying factor in the face of continued revolutionary turmoil.

On the morning of 27 May, the SDC – including Khamenei, Rafsanjani, Defence Minister Major General Mohamad Salimi, Zahirnejhad, Shirazi and Rezai – went to Khomeini's home and it was later announced that 'certain decisions' had been made. In fact Khomeini at first backed the conservatives but then Rafsanjani and Rezai began to meet him separately, bringing with them exiled Iraqi Shias, including Hojatolislam Mohammad Bakir al-Hakim who led the Supreme Assembly of the Islamic Revolution in Iraq (SCIRI).

Hakim had created the guerrilla Badr Brigades which had struck army supply centres in Iraq during the May 1982 offensive.[2] Hakim claimed the Shia were waiting to rise the moment Iranian forces crossed the frontier and would clear the way for the invaders. The radicals also reminded Khomeini that if left unchallenged, the enemy could rebuild their forces and again threaten Iran. To prevent this Iran had to carry the war to the enemy until the secular Ba'athist regime was defeated and overthrown.

Mulling these arguments, Khomeini began to waver and decided in favour of the offensive, probably on 20 June, for the next day he announced: 'We shall get to Lebanon, and to Jerusalem, through Iraq, but first we have to defeat the sinister Ba'ath party', while a popular revolutionary refrain claimed: 'The road to Jerusalem passes through Karbala'. Ominously for Saddam, Iraqi Shiites began rioting in Baghdad and despite the expulsion of 100,000 their resistance organisation, Daawa, attempted to assassinate the Iraqi leader at Dujayal on 11 July.

Two days earlier Rafsanjani listed Tehran's terms for ending the war; acceptance of the Algiers Agreement of 1975, repatriation of 100,000 expelled Iraqi Shias, acceptance by Iraq of responsibility for the war, US$100 billion in reparations and Saddam to be tried as a war criminal. The terms were clearly unacceptable and, fearing a continuation of the conflict, the UN Security Council on 12 July passed a resolution calling for a ceasefire and a withdrawal of forces to their borders, but by then the Iranians were completing their final preparations.[3] However, Khomeini's insistence that the SDC avoid heavily populated areas to avoid heavy casualties among the Iraqi Shia limited their options. Hakim would accompany the Iranian forces to encourage a rising and help the Pasdaran win them over. But this Fifth Column never emerged, for as with the Sunni Arabs of Khuzestan, the inhabitants generally regarded themselves as Iraqis first and Shias second.

The 1,700-kilometre-long front offered few weak points which might prove lethal to Saddam's regime. Mountains barred progress to the northern oil fields, but Kurdish desire for autonomy could be exploited to harass exports through Turkey and force the dictator to maintain large numbers of troops in the region. In the centre, Iran's poor road network saw general logistics issues restrain any drive into the Sunni heartland of Iraq by restricting the assembly of troops, which left the southern front as the best strategic level option. The prize was Basra, the capital of a Shia region which held much of Iran's hydrocarbon wealth, but it was also a region which held a major concentration of Iranian forces with the best communications network in the country.

The first campaigns here would be fought south of the Hawizah Marshes (Hawr al-Hawizah) in a knife-shaped stretch of land some 55 kilometres long and 45 kilometres at its widest point. The straight edge was the international border in the east while the Shatt al-Arab, known to the Iranians as the River Arvand, was the edge of the 'blade' which curved gently eastward on its way to the Gulf. Within the 'blade' and south of the Ghuzail, an area of desolate salt flats and sand just south of the marshes, the ground rose imperceptibly to act as a land bridge between the marshes and the coastal salt flats.

Much of this ground consisted of desert, criss-crossed with earth roads on embankments or berms but the high water table, up to 3 centimetres, meant they could become marshy during the winter rains, although in summer, according to British Army maps of 1943, the ground was firm enough to allow 1.5-tonne trucks to drive at speeds 'up to 40 mph' (74 km/h). Earth roads criss-crossed the desert to provide a degree of all-weather communications while along the northern bank of the Shatt lay a major metalled (hard top) highway linking Basra to Khorammshahr. To the south, the banks of the Shatt up to 4 kilometres wide are extensively cultivated, dotted with palm groves, and criss-crossed by irrigation ditches. Within the Shatt itself lay numerous small islands which would play a greater role in later operations.

The dominating feature was the so-called Fish Lake (Buhayrat al-Asmak, called Kanal Mahi by the Iranians) some 15 kilometres northeast of Basra. This was a 30 kilometre-long flooded anti-armour ditch, built in the late 1970s to split an Iranian offensive,

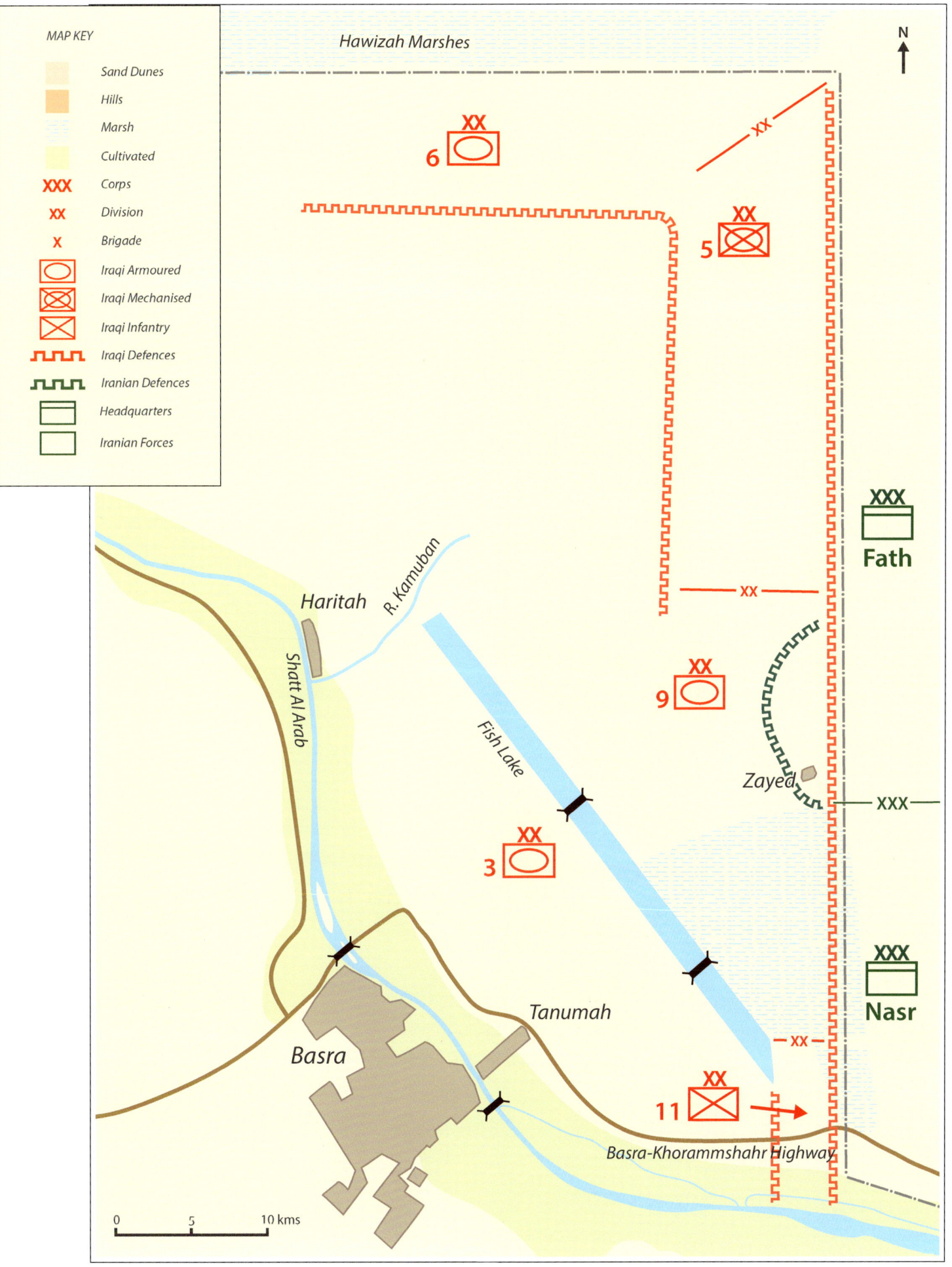

Map 1: Operation Ramadan Mubarak

and it was 1.25 kilometres wide, up to 3 metres deep, with water pumped in from the Shatt through irrigation channels and dedicated pumps.[4] On the west bank of the lake was a berm 1.5 metres high and 10 metres wide, from which defenders could cover the waters and the two causeways which crossed them to launch counter-attacks. Across the lake there was an embankment with an earth road running from near the Shatt to Hoseyniyeh on the Ahwaz-Khorammshahr highway and railway in Iran. From the northern end of the Lake there was a potential obstacle or switch line in the River Kamuban (Katiban or Kutayban) which ran westward to the Shatt which it enters 14 kilometres north of Basra.

As the Iraqi occupation began to crumble, around April 1982, work began upon defences around the Fish Lake to shield Basra. The work was directed and planned by the corps engineer commander, Brigadier Adnan Hussein Makki, and executed as a state engineering or State Central Effort (Jahd ad-Dawla al-Markzi), by his battalions, civilian contractors and labour, together with drafted civilians provided by the Mayor of Basra – who was responsible for the State Central Effort. The plans were drawn up by the corps then sent for approval to the Defence Ministry's Planning Directorate. Once approved, the army would build the field fortifications while the civilians would produce the communications and rear fortifications.

The first task was to build a berm-based defensive line from the southern edge of the Fish Lake across the Basra-Khorramshahr highway, because the high water table made trenches deeper than waist or shoulder height impractical. Three battalion-strongpoints were built, and by mid-July work had begun upon a second and a third berm line behind the first, the third acting as a switch position west of the Lake. To divide an advance, lake water was allowed to spill out opposite its central section to flood terrain several kilometres wide to the east up to, and beyond, the border.

Yet the Iraqi defences were mostly along the frontier for, like most politicians and dictators, Saddam was loathed to surrender territory because it eroded his personal prestige. On each side of the flooded area an anti-armour ditch some

Mohsen Rezai (centre left, with a cap), leading Iranian war planner and battlefield commander during the mid-1980s. (Tom Cooper Collection)

A group of officers from the 92nd Armoured Division IRIA clustering around a M577 armoured command post. Such vehicles played an important role as mobile communication centres and for directing artillery fire. (Tom Cooper Collection)

90 kilometres long was dug along the border, and the excavated earth and sand was used to construct a 2.25-4 metre high berm which would be the forward element of the defences. This berm was the basis for triangular battalion-strongpoints with triangular company-strongpoints sited for all-round defence in each angle, two in the forward wall some 2 kilometres apart, with a third a kilometre behind, all linked by berms about 1.9-2 metres high.[5] Some of these positions were built upon the sites of former border guard installations.

At each corner of the fortification would be a fire position with reinforced-concrete walls and overhead cover, linked by trenches along the berm tops; the men living in trenches or dugouts. The walls of the berm were an easily-scalable 45 degree angle, but were studded with wire and mines and covered with fire positions within the berm wall and outside it. The berm fire positions had excellent fields of fire over deep and dense obstacle fields; with anti-armour and anti-personnel mines as well as barbed wire and razor wire entanglements between the berm and the anti-armour ditch. Along the ditch was a screening force both to prevent raids and provide early warning of imminent assault; with each brigade deploying a platoon, while in front of this were company-size guard forces, although along the northern face of the defences the 6th Armoured Division reconnaissance regiment provided the equivalent of a battalion. The Iraqis also decided upon a tactical experiment in which the screening forces were augmented by an Offensive Delaying Force (Quwat at-Taweek at-Taaruthia) consisting of platoon or company-strongpoints on the flanks of potential axes of advance in order to disrupt the advance before withdrawing, with the screening force, to the Main Line of Resistance (MLR).

A rifle platoon of Pasdaran squatting on the ground while being briefed for their next mission. Most are armed with AK-47 assault rifles, either captured from the Iraqis or purchased from China. (Albert Grandolini Collection)

An Iranian armoured battalion equipped with M47Ms, probably from the 77th Infantry Division, seen while moving out at the start of the Operation Ramadan Mubarak. (Mark Lepko Collection)

The Iraqi Army staff had finally persuaded Saddam of the value of defence-in-depth, so their forces were deployed in echelon. The battle interrupted work on a berm which was to be the basis of a new back-stop defensive system covering the north-eastern segment of the Fish Lake, up to 10 kilometres from the northern border and 25 kilometres from the eastern, which was used largely to shelter artillery and armoured reserves. Separate positions covered by berms were used to shelter batteries and reserve armoured/mechanised forces while work began on a road network to the Basra railhead.

Although IRIAF RF-4Es are known to have flown up to a dozen reconnaissance sorties over the operational zone, and although it

A volley of rockets fired from an Iraqi BM-21 Grad MRLS. Both sides used this Soviet-made truck-mounted system in large numbers for area attacks. The BM-21 proved devastating against exposed infantry and quite valuable in destroying defences in counter-battery work. (Tom Cooper Collection)

Two AH-1 Cobras with a Bell 214A Esfahan (background) of the IRIAA in the process of taking off from a forward operating location. Iranian Army Aviation deployed one tactical group with 34 attack and transport helicopters in support of Operation Ramadan Mubarak. (Tom Cooper Collection)

is known that two of the IRIAF's C-130E Khofaash SIGINT-gatherers were reading Iraqi military communications in real time, it is unclear how much the IRIA knew of these defences when outline planning for what became Operation 'Ramadan al-Mubarak' (Blessed Ramadan) began in June, but it appears to have been limited. At least one Pasdaran source indicates the reconnaissance was found wanting.[6] The work probably began as a contingency plan which the inexperienced IRIA staff officers no doubt hoped – given the condition of their forces – would not have to be executed. Their hopes probably began to fade from mid June when it became obvious the SDC was slowly swinging towards an offensive. Detailed planning probably did not begin until late June or early July as the IRIAF's reconnaissance aircraft flew more sorties over the potential battlefield.

Once again General Rahim Safavi, the mastermind of the Beit-ol-Moqaddas triumph, would plan the operation, although the IRIA remained under a cloud following the Ghotbzadeh Plot (for both events see Volume 1). US intelligence calculated that Safavi had 150,000 men and intended to strike north of the Fish Lake; punch a hole through the MLR and then push an armoured spearhead around the north of the lake through Harithah to a distance of 30 kilometres; cross the River Kamuban and then circle behind the lake to link up at Tanumah opposite Basra.[7] There it would link up with a secondary thrust which would advance 15 kilometres along the Abadan-Basra highway and together they would swarm into the city.[8]

Essentially the Iranians intended to bulldoze their way through the defences with a frontal-assault westwards and would not try to split the defenders through an assault from the north. This may reflect a lack of intelligence at a time when the Iranians wrongly assumed that the Iraqi forces were still in turmoil after the recent defeats in Khuzestan. A major problem for the Iranians was that they launched their offensive only 50 days after taking Khorramshahr, leaving little time for the Pasdaran to replace losses in men and equipment, although the IRIA had the advantage of a well-established replacement organisation which could provide ad hoc Qods (Jerusalem) battalions. There were also problems with supplies as the Ahwaz-Khorramshahr rail line had been badly damaged during the Iraqi occupation, with much of the rail bed and rails removed to create fortifications, and the line was still being repaired when 'Ramadan' was launched.

The operation would be directed by the Ahwaz-based Southern Forward Operations Headquarters (SFOH) – also known as Karbala – but following their success in Beit-ol-Mogaddas, tactical control was assigned to the task forces (Gharargah); once temporary command groupings but now permanent professional organisations. Operations north of the flooded area were conducted by Task Force

Fath, under Colonel Niaki, while those south of the area would be conducted by Task Force Nasr; a total of some 76,000 men, including 37,000 Pasdaran and Basiji. Niaki had a mechanised brigade of the 16th Armoured Division (IRIA, but reinforced by the 40th Sarab Infantry Brigade, IRGC), the 77th Infantry Division (IRIA) teamed with the 1st Qods and 7th Vali Asr Infantry Divisions of the IRGC, and two brigades (1st Mechanised and 4th Armoured) of 92nd Armoured Division teamed with the 3rd Saheb ol-Zamen Infantry Division (IRGC). Nasr's offensive would be launched by the 21st Infantry Division (IRIA, but reinforced by a tank battalion and a special forces battalion) and 5th Nasr Infantry Division reinforced by elements of the 30th Beit-ol-Moghaddas Armoured Division (both IRGC). However, Ramadan al-Mubarak was hamstrung by a shortage of material; between them the armoured formations had only 200 tanks, the lion's share with the 92nd Division.

This was the first offensive in which the Pasdaran used armour, concentrated within the 30th 'Beit-ol-Moghaddas' Division, which began to receive captured T-55 MBTs, together with BMP-1 infantry fighting vehicles (IFVs), and Chinese Type-63 armoured personnel carriers (APCs), although its operational armour consisted only of one or two battalions of second-hand IRIA M47 Pattons. In fact none of the army divisions was complete, apparently deploying no more than two brigades each, while the 22nd and 33rd Artillery Groups had six battalions of M109 self-propelled 155mm howitzers, three batteries of M107 175mm self-propelled guns, nine battalions of towed guns and two batteries (about a dozen) of Multiple Rocket Launcher Systems (MRLS) – in total some 270 tubes. Yet during the Operation Beit-ol-Mogaddas, barely two months earlier, the Iranians had deployed some 20 artillery battalions with more than 300 guns and 40 MRLS, as well as 350 MBTs, an ominous drop in

Iraqi tanks also suffered from Iranian attack helicopters: this T-62 was bogged down in the mud and then hit by a BGM-71 TOW, which then caused a typical conflagration that flipped the turret on the side. (Tom Cooper Collection)

Ramadan Mubarak was often fought in fierce sand storms, which explain why these two Iraqi T-62s came to get bogged down and trapped in what appears to be an Iraqi anti-armour ditch. (Tom Cooper Collection)

the level of support. Further support was provided by the Islamic Republic Iran Army Aviation (IRIAA), the army air corps had assembled 34 Bell AH-1J Cobra attack helicopters augmented by Bell 204s, Bell 206s, Bell 214s, and Boeing CH-47 Chinooks in the support role. The Islamic Republic of Iran Air Force (IRIAF) had lost some 120 aircraft in the past 18 months but still had some 250 combat aircraft. Much of the fleet was undergoing overhauls, badly needed after massive battles for the liberation of Khuzestan, and there was some lack of ammunition too, but even more serious was the lack of experienced crews caused by losses early during the war. Correspondingly, the IRIAF was forced to husband its resources and limit involvement in offensive operations.[9]

In May 1981, the Soviet Union began selling arms to Iraq again. One of the first orders Baghdad placed was for additional T-72s, multiple shipments of which reached the port of Aqaba in Jordan by the end of the same year. Several T-72s can be seen while in the process of deploying east of Basra, about a year later. (Tom Cooper Collection)

Still from a video taken in summer 1982, showing an Iraqi Mi-25 in the process of launching an AT-2 Swatter ATGM. (Iraqi National TV capture)

Pasdaran operations with the IRIA were co-ordinated by their deputy military commander, Yahya Rahim Safavi, repeating the successful arrangements during Beit-ol-Moqaddas, and they would play a major role in the offensive together with the National Mobilisation Organisation (Sazman-e Basij-e Milli) or Basij. By now many Pasdaran leaders were battle-scarred veterans, yet there remained a hard core of leaders who were brave but functionally illiterate and who saw little point in intricately prepared plans.

Further hurdles for the Iranian troops were meteorological and spiritual. In April the clerics pressed for the early liberation of Khuzestan and argued that it would be impossible during the blazing summer months, yet they were now so anxious to take the war to Iraq that they demanded an attack during July. This would mean fighting in open desert under cloudless skies in temperatures normally reaching up to 120° F or 49° C.[10] Worse, the fighting would take place during the holy month of Ramadan al-Mubarak (23 June–22 July), which gave its name to the offensive, during which Moslems are expected to fast and avoid water during the daylight hours. Followers may receive exemption in severe physical or meteorological conditions but it is unclear whether or not the clerics gave the assault troops dispensation, without it the Iranians would rapidly face exhaustion.

Across the frontier, the defending III Corps had been in a state of frantic, almost chaotic, activity in the aftermath of Beit-ol-Mogaddas. The former commander, General Salah al-Qadhi was arrested in June, court-martialled the following month for the loss of Khuzestan and Khorramshahr, and executed. He was replaced by Major General Sa'adi Tumma al-Juburi whose chief of staff was Brigadier Aladdin Hussein Makki Khamas (who stood in no relation to the corps' engineer chief). Unlike so many senior officers in the Iraqi Army, these were extremely capable and experienced staff officers who would play key roles in reforming the army.[11] Immediately they conducted a personal reconnaissance of the front, familiarising themselves with the divisions' conditions, following which Makki drew up an operational plan incorporating the latest intelligence in which the divisional commanders were briefed to fight a defence-in-depth with the frontier berm line as the MLR. Prompt counter-attacks were to squeeze out any penetrations of the MLR and an armoured reaction force would prevent any major break-through by a co-ordinated counter-attack with heavy artillery and air support.[12]

However, the Iraqi Army was still recovering from the battering it had received in the spring when it was reduced to 150,000 men and two armoured divisions were reduced to brigade strength.[13] The army was being rapidly rebuilt and expanded by combing out those previously excluded from conscription and by drafting in more Popular Army (al-Jaysh ah-Shabi) Ba'ath Party militia and transferring more para-military forces from the Police and Border Guards. It was easier to replace the large amounts of equipment lost in Iran through the renewal of Soviet arms sales in 1981, augmented by Egyptian Army surplus equipment of East European origin, the newly opened supply line from China, and deliveries from non-Communist countries, especially Brazil and France.

In the aftermath of the disaster at Khorramshahr there were significant changes in the Iraqi Army. Saddam is reported to have dismissed 200-300 officers, and executed some, replacing them with those who had demonstrated ability. The crisis meant that ability temporarily became the criterion, with less of the rotation of division and corps commanders intended to prevent them from challenging the regime. However, personal ties with Saddam, such as marriage, coming from his birthplace of Tikrit, or having close tribal affiliations also helped. By the end of the war, senior officers including Generals Maher, Rashid, Shaban and Director of State

Intelligence (Mukhabarat) al-Barrak, were all members of Saddam's Albu Nasr clan.[14] This growing professionalism led to a reappraisal of Iraqi Army doctrine, which led to a greater reliance upon defence-in-depth and the use of mobile reserves of mechanised and special forces, together with more patrolling and probing of enemy positions; a US intelligence report later noting that Iraqi commanders displayed 'greater skill and imagination in the conduct of the defence' aided by improved air and artillery support.[15]

The backbone of the defence remained the same formations which had failed to hold Khuzestan; 3rd, 6th and 9th Armoured Divisions, 5th Mechanised Division and 11th Infantry Division – all of which had been battered to a greater or lesser extent in the debacle – augmented by 10th Armoured Guards based in Basra and 33rd Special Forces Brigade. These were stationed behind the Fish Lake beside the HQ of the 3rd Armoured Division. Generous leave arrangements meant the defenders had some 85,000 men, 1,300 MBTs, 490 guns (81 batteries), three mortar units with 240mm tubes, and a MRLS regiment with 60 122mm BM-21 Grad (Hail) weapon systems, possibly augmented by launchers aboard the Project 771-class (ASCC/NATO-code 'Polnocny-B') landing ships rusting in the Basra naval base. Six artillery batteries remained under corps command, while another six were assigned to III Corps' 15th Infantry Division on the south bank of the Shatt and the Faw Peninsula to interdict the enemy on the other side of the waterway.[16]

Some of the divisions were under new commanders, such as 11th Infantry Division (nominally in command of Khorramshahr as of May 1982), although Brigadier Said Mohammad Fethi's

Because they proved vulnerable to small-arms fire, SA.342 Gazelles usually followed Mi-25s into the attack, and fired their HOT anti-tank missiles from stand-off ranges. (Tom Cooper Collection)

headquarters were in Iraq at the time. Fethi, a competent although plodding officer, was not held accountable for its loss and in late June was transferred to command a Border Guards division, being replaced by Major General Mohammad Abdul Qadir. This former 15th Infantry Division commander was a clever, dynamic and brilliant leader who quickly reorganised his forces and turned their fortifications into model defensive positions to block the Basra-Khorramshahr highway. He had eight infantry brigades, positioned – from north to south – as follows: 109th, 49th, 45th, 22nd, 47th, 48th, 38th, and 502nd. The 12th Armoured Brigade reinforced by a tank battalion from the 6th Armoured Brigade, 18 artillery batteries with 78 guns and some MRLS completed his order of battle (ORBAT). On the northern side was 6th Armoured Division under Major General Mahmood Shukur Shahin who had demonstrated competence under fire in Iran. Shukur had (west to east), 11th Border Guard, 56th Armoured, 16th Armoured, 25th Mechanised

Table 1: IRIA/IRGC, Southern Forward Operations HQ (Karbala HQ), July 1982

Corps	Division & HQ	Brigades & Notes
	Direct Combat Support Group (IRIAA)	1 Attack Battalion (AH-1Js), 1 Assault Battalion (Bell 214As), 1 Reconnaissance Battalion (Bell 206), 1 Transport Battalion (CH-47C)
	22nd Artillery Group (Esfahan)	3 battalions of M109; 2 batteries of M107; 3 battalions of towed artillery pieces; 1 MRLS battalion (total of about 100 artillery pieces and 12 BM-21s)
	33rd Artillery Group (Tehran)	3 battalions of M109; 1 battery of M107; 4 battalions of towed artillery pieces; 1 MRLS battalion (total of about 100 artillery pieces and 12 BM-21s)
Task Force Fath	16th Armoured Division (IRIA)	1 armoured brigade only; reinforced by 40th Sarab Brigade (IRGC)
	77th Infantry Division (IRIA)	
	92nd Armoured Division	1st Mechanized and 4th Armoured Brigades only
	1st Qods Division (IRGC)	
	3rd Saheb al-Zamen Division (IRGC)	
	7th Vali Asr Division (IRGC)	
Task Force Nasr	21st Infantry Division (IRIA)	reinforced by 1 tank battalion and 1 SF-battalion
	30th Beit-ol-Moghaddas Armoured Division (IRGC)	

Iraqi attack helicopters caused heavy losses to inexperienced tankers of the IRGC in summer 1982. This BMP-1 was knocked out by an ATGM-hit and had its turret blown away. The open hatch at the rear might indicate that some of the crew managed to escape. (Tom Cooper Collection)

and 94th Infantry Brigades and in reserve 30th Armoured Brigade, although this could be reinforced by III Corps' 10th Armoured Brigade – equipped with T-72 Main Battle Tanks (MBTs). For fire support he had 12 batteries with 72 tubes (including nine self-propelled 2S1 Gvozdika 122mm howitzers).

The eastern face of the defences, which would face the brunt of the attacks, consisted of Brigadier Maher Abdul Rashid's 5th Mechanised Division, Brigadier Khudaier Abbas Al-Khathban's 9th Armoured Division and Brigadier Hussein Rashid's 3rd Armoured Division, the last straddling the Fish Lake. Both Abdul Rashid and Hussein Rashid were from Saddam's home town of Tikrit, while Khathban was a Shi'a commander who owed much to his Ba'athist credentials. Maher Rashid had 26th and 55th Armoured, 15th and 20th Mechanised as well as 419th Infantry Brigades, with 18 batteries and more than 100 guns, a few batteries of MRLS and a dozen 120mm mortars. Khathban had 35th and 43rd Armoured, 14th Mechanised and 104th Infantry Brigades, supported by nine batteries (36 guns) and MRLS, while Hussein Rashid's 3rd Armoured Division controlled the 6th Armoured, 8th Mechanised, 418th and 504th Infantry Brigades and a dozen batteries with 54 guns.

The Iraqis had been reading enemy radio communications since the spring of 1982 which provided a good idea of their intentions, although because the Pasdaran lacked radios and communicated largely by landline or messenger, Baghdad was unsure of overall enemy strength. Sa'adi's men were certainly on the alert from early July as enemy artillery preparation increased especially from 12 July, while Iraqi Communications Intelligence (COMINT) monitored the airways for the enemy signal which would begin the offensive. These signals tended to be words or phrases from the Koran, a practise called in Farsi 'estekhareh' and in English 'bibliomancy', although references to Shia saints were also included.[17]

On the evening of 13 July the Iranians broadcast the code phrase 'Thou absent Imam! Thou absent Imam!' (Ya Saheb ez-Zaman! Ya Saheb ez-Zaman!) – and at 2210 hrs the Iranians began to move out as III Corps alerted its formations and decided to bring the T-72s of the 10th Armoured Brigade across the Shatt during the evening. Saddam was also informed and sent as his representative Izzat Ibrahim ad-Duri, vice chairman of the Revolutionary Command Council (RCC), the Ba'ath Party equivalent of the Soviet Politburo, to Sa'adi's headquarters 'to raise morale' and also to act as Saddam's unwelcome eyes.

Table 2: III Corps Iraqi Army, 1982

Division	Brigades and Notes
3rd Armoured Division	6th Armoured Brigade; 8th Mechanised Brigade; 418th and 504th Infantry Brigades; 12 artillery batteries
5th Mechanised Division	26th and 55th Armoured Brigades; 15th and 20th Mechanised Brigades; 419th Infantry Brigade; 18 artillery and MRLS batteries
6th Armoured Division	11th Border Guard Brigade; 16th, 30th and 56th Armoured Brigades; 25th Mechanised Brigade; 94th Infantry Brigade
9th Armoured Division	35th and 43rd Armoured Brigades; 14th Mechanised and 104th Infantry Brigades; 9 artillery and MRLS batteries
11th Infantry Division	22nd, 38th, 45th, 47th, 48th, 49th, 109th, 502nd Infantry Brigades; 12th Armoured Brigade; battalion from 6th Armoured Brigade; 18 artillery batteries
reserve forces	10th Armoured Brigade
reserve forces	33rd SF Brigade

Table 3: Known Units of the Iraqi Army Aviation Corps (IrAAC), 1982-1984

Unit	Helicopter Type
No. 2 Squadron	Mi-8/17
No. 4 Squadron	Mi-8/17
No. 12 Squadron	Mi-8/17
No. 15 Squadron	Mi-8/17
No. 21 Squadron	SA.342 Gazelle
No. 22 Squadron	SA.342 Gazelle
No. 25 Squadron	Mi-25
No. 30 Squadron	SE.316B
No. 31 Squadron	SA.342 Gazelle
No. 55 Squadron	Mi-8/17
No. 61 Squadron	Mi-25
No. 66 Squadron	Mi-25
No. 84 Squadron	SA.342 Gazelle
No. 88 Squadron	SA.342 Gazelle

First Offensive 13–14 July

The Iranians advanced along much of the front, with Task Force Nasr hitting 11th Infantry Division on the Iraqi right. This diversion appears to have inflicted heavy casualties on Qadir's 49th Infantry Brigade, although this brigade still prevented them from reaching the eastern bank of the Fish Lake and eliminated the Iranian presence in the morning. The main assault was made by Task Force Fath on a 10 kilometre front opposite the northern Fish Lake, extending from 5th Mechanised Division's 20th Mechanised Brigade to 3rd Armoured Division's 418th Infantry Brigade; but, the main blow – by 92nd Armoured Division reinforced by Saheb al-Zaman and Vali Asr – exploited a small bridgehead previously established along the frontier around the Iraqi frontier post at Zayed (also Said, Seid, Zaid or Zeid) opposite 9th Armoured Division's sector, to strike its two forward units: the 104th Infantry and 14th Mechanised Brigades.

The Iranian bridgehead allowed IRIA engineers to secretly clear paths through the obstacle fields. When the attack began this eased the passage of the infantry led by the Basiji, who sometimes accidentally strayed off the paths to inadvertently act as human minesweepers. They and the Pasdaran moved forward, with armoured units up to a kilometre behind them, and quickly pushed back the screening forces as the bombardment fell. When it lifted they were able to swarm up the berms and claimed they took many strongpoints within 90 minutes, although Tehran later stated it had only 600 prisoners. IRIA engineers bulldozed gaps in the berms to allow armour and motorised troops, the latter including Pasdaran in Toyota pick-up trucks, automobiles and even motorcycles, to sweep westwards supported by 92nd Division's Chieftains and mechanised infantry battalions. Part of this force reached the Fish Lake, but they lacked the means to cross it and some units were isolated by counter-attacks and had a hard time fighting their way back to friendly territory.

Soon after midnight they encountered 9th Armoured Division's reserve (35th and 43rd Armoured Brigades), still largely in their fortified laagers, which the Iranians infiltrated in order to reach and to overrun Khathban's headquarters and capture his Mercedes-Benz limousine, which was a gift from Saddam. The two armoured brigades made a hasty withdrawal, with 43rd Brigade moving west to the newly constructed berm around the gap between its southern edge and the Fish Lake, while the 35th Brigade retreated southwards to one of the Fish Lake crossing points from where it desperately resisted.

To the north 77th and Qods Divisions had struck Abdul Rashid's 5th Mechanised Division some 15 minutes before the main blow. They emulated the early success of their southern neighbours and pushed through 20th Mechanised and 419th Infantry Brigades, but Abdul Rashid's counter-attacks by the well-placed 26th and 55th Armoured Brigades prevented them striking northwards. Niaki's spearheads did advance some 25 kilometres to the west but fierce resistance from Rashid's armour and Khathban's surviving brigades prevented them circling around the northern Fish Lake. Nevertheless the success was sufficient to attract part of 21st Division northwards to help exploit it.

As dawn approached, the Pasdaran and Basiji began to consolidate their hold, but the IRIA were already suffering major supply problems which might have been exacerbated if Iraqi air power had

Crew of an Iraqi OT-62 stretching their legs during a break in fighting. The losses of 1982, and re-opening of supply-lines to Moscow, resulted in the early demise of this venerable and reliable mount, and its replacement with BMP-1s. (Albert Grandolini Collection)

The Iranian 77th Infantry Division assaulted the northern end of Iraqi border defences during Operation Ramadan Mubarak. Casualties were heavy and included this BMP-1 and two MBTs (type unrecognizable), which became trapped in the anti-armour ditch and were then knocked out. (Tom Cooper Collection)

The crew of an Iraqi T-72 from the 10th Armoured Brigade posing at the rear of their vehicle. This unit played a key role in spearheading counter-attacks against Ramadan Mubarak and generally acting as a fire-brigade. (Albert Grandolini Collection)

Both sides acquired hundreds of tank-transporters before the war: the Iraqis ended the conflict possessing more than 1,000 of such vehicles, which enabled them to move an entire armoured division from one portion of the frontline to the other in as little as 24 hours. This US-made Mack is hauling an IRGC-operated T-54/55 to the frontline. (Albert Grandolini Collection)

not been largely grounded by a sandstorm. The Pasdaran and Basiji depots were receiving food from the regions or mosques, while ammunition from the Pasdaran Ministry was received in fits and starts.[18] The militias were soon running out of essentials, while the rudimentary command and control system meant spearheads were stuck on their first objective unless one of the more dynamic leaders personally led them beyond. Worse still, while they might dig foxholes for personal safety, they rarely created a defensive system with obstacles, interlocking fields of fire and access to artillery or even air support, features which were abundant in the Iraqi defences.

The situation by morning was critical but neither Sa'adi nor Makki panicked, despite losing touch with Khathban, while the other divisional commanders also kept their heads and fed III Corps headquarters a steady stream of reports. Within five hours they had built up an accurate picture of the situation and were determined to launch an armoured riposte under Shukur, whose 30th Armoured Brigade was reinforced by the newly-arrived 10th and 16th Armoured Brigades, withdrawn from the forward defences.

At dawn on 14 July, Sa'adi and Makki left the operations officer at divisional headquarters and set out from III Corps headquarters, with a small command team, for 6th Armoured Division headquarters. As they drove eastwards there was a scare when small arms fire was heard from the Fish Lake where elements of 21st Division had established a presence on its banks. Makki quickly organized troops to contain this threat – the newly arrived 5th Mountain Brigade was diverted to meet it by Qadir's headquarters – while Sa'adi drove on to meet Shukur.

Iranian aircraft observed the Iraqi concentration but could do little more than warn of the impending threat as the sandstorm denied each side air support by reducing visibility to a few metres. The attack by 350 tanks began at 0945 hrs, after a short bombardment possibly including CS (O-Chlororbenzyl-malononitrile) tear gas.[19] The Iranians lacked gas masks and suffered streaming eyes and raucous coughs which undermined the resolve of men who would normally and enthusiastically charge through sheets of bullets and showers of shells. Meanwhile, Shukur's two brigades drove out from the gap between the new berm and the Fish Lake, with their right secured by the Fish Lake, while 10th Brigade advanced from the eastern side of the new berm, its left secured by 5th Mechanised Division, as fierce fighting developed.

In good visibility the outnumbered Iranian Chieftain tank-killers would have given a better account of themselves because they were superior to everything except the T-72, but swirling dust clouds imposed a double penalty. The tank's fire control system, which was superior to anything in a Soviet-designed MBT, was neutralised as both sides pounded each other at point-blank range, while the dust aggravated the British tank's weak point, its notoriously unreliable L60 engine which tended to overheat, especially when the filters were clogged with fine dust. The gun stabilisation system was so unreliable that the crews had stopped repairing them and preferred to hang a heavy stone under the breach to keep the gun in a horizontal position.[20]

Many vehicles broke down and had to be abandoned, while many crews owed their lives to the 'wet storage' of the bagged combustible charges (which were in cells surrounded by pressurised water and glycol). If the cells were penetrated, the charges would be saturated, to make a distinctive sizzling sound and emit white smoke, giving the crew several minutes to bale out, often with wounded men.[21] The Iranians still accounted for many MBTs, many of which fought private battles, before the survivors were gradually pushed westwards and, ultimately, across the border. The RPG teams, who were often on motorcycles, were hindered by a shortage of ammunition, each member of the two- or three-man teams carrying only three rounds, and their commanders had demanded they be used economically. They were to use them only when they were certain they would hit an AFV, which meant approaching to as little as 200 metres, a task which required a great deal of skill and luck. When their RPGs were expended, some men tried to board the tanks to throw a grenade inside, but few succeeded and losses were high. The Iranians would claim 85 AFVs, but the infantry – especially the Pasdaran and Basiji, already reeling from gas – was caught in the open desert and slaughtered with one Iranian tank commander later claiming that 70% of the volunteers attached to his unit were dead by midday.[22]

An Iranian Army TOW-team, mounted on a M141 MUTT jeep, approaching a sector of frontline held by the IRGC, along the highway connecting Khorramshahr with Basra. (Tom Cooper Collection)

The divisions of the regular Iranian Army retired in good order to the former Iraqi forward defences, which they still held, and there followed a pause during the night, but the Iraqis renewed their assault on the frontier defences during the morning and by the end of the day regained the lost positions. Defence Minister and Deputy Commander-in-Chief, Major General Adnan Khairallah Talfah, who was flying over the battlefield, brought some of the first reports of an enemy retreat. His actions were extremely brave but foolhardy, for his helicopter was frequently fired upon by his own troops, leading Sa'adi to admonish his men not to fire upon friendly aircraft. Helicopters were later used to fly crews forward to recover enemy vehicles.[23]

A feature of this offensive was Iraq's use on the battlefield of the Soviet Mi-25 (ASCC/NATO-code 'Hind') armoured helicopters, with a combat radius of some 225 kilometres.[24] At the start of the war the IrAAC had only seven, and five were lost in the next four months, and with Afghanistan given priority for these aircraft by Moscow, replacements were slow to arrive, so that by August 1982 only 20 were operational. Until the summer of 1982 they were used to carry reaction forces to counter commando raids on important installations such as radar stations, being described by the Iraqis as 'combat transports.' With East German assistance during the summer, they were integrated into conventional operations, working as teams with the Gazelles, five such teams being organised. The 'Hinds' would lead the anti-armour aircraft and suppress air defences with unguided rockets and a 12.7mm Gatling gun, allowing the Gazelles to exploit the enemy's confusion and use HOT anti-tank guided missiles (ATGM) to pick off individual AFVs. The 'Hind' was built to carry up to four 9K17 Skorpion (ASCC/NATO-code 'AT-2B Swatter') radio-guided missiles, with a 2.5 kilometre range, and 1,000 were delivered with the aircraft. Although expended in considerable numbers they proved ineffective against Chieftains. Curiously, Soviet advisors noted these formidable helicopters rarely carried these weapons, while US Army Intelligence noted the 'Hinds' were still being used 'to move both men and equipment to critical spots'.[25]

The Iranian attack had been held, but it was a very close thing and the Iraqis had suffered heavy casualties, with about half 9th Armoured Division destroyed together with 5th Mechanised Division's 20th Mechanised Brigade. The Iraqis had been forced to commit almost all their armoured reserve, much of which now had to hold the forward defences. The need to replace units saw I Corps ordered to transfer 8th Infantry Division and most of 12th Armoured Division (37th Armoured and 46th Mechanised Brigades) as well as 4th Mountain, 5th Mountain and 18th Infantry Brigades, while II Corps' 10th Armoured Division lost its 24th Mechanised Brigade, and the 1st Mechanised Division lost the 34th Armoured Brigade. Also sent south were 53rd Armoured, 427th and 602nd Infantry Brigades. The Iranians had also suffered badly, with 92nd Division losing some 100 AFVs, but they had the manpower to continue.

Second Offensive July 16

On the morning of 16 July, Makki debriefed the divisional commanders and in a meeting lasting until noon they refined their plans while engineers feverishly worked to turn the second berm line into a succession of strongpoints. Yet the situation remained critical, for Sa'adi had been forced to commit his whole mechanized reserve and until reinforcements arrived there remained a hole in the former 9th Armoured Division sector. Abdul Rashid's badly battered 15th Mechanised Brigade had had to be withdrawn for rest and re-organisation, leaving Shurkur's 30th Armoured Brigade and

GHQ's 10th Armoured Brigade now in the line on each side of the 5th Mechanised/9th Armoured Division boundary, Shukur's 20th Mechanised Brigade was next in line, while Khathban's surviving 43rd and 35th Armoured Brigades held 9th Armoured Division's right. With Shukur's 26th Armoured Brigade pressed to hold his line, the only armoured reserve uncommitted was his 16th and 55th Armoured Brigades.

Niaki recognized he had come close to success and after an intensive IRIAF reconnaissance effort which undoubtedly revealed the enemy's lack of reserves, he decided to exploit his previous success with a renewed assault upon 9th Armoured Division's sector. He struck on the night of 16/17 July, again spearheaded by 77th Division supported by the battered Pasdaran formations and a brigade of 92nd Division. The defenders lacked infantry to hold the weakened and battered strongpoints, there were only half-a-dozen infantry battalions to hold the whole 9th Armoured Division sector, so once again the forward positions were quickly lost. But when the Iranians reached the open ground they were slowed by heavy artillery fire and stopped by the mechanized formations. Inevitably, the Iranians' greatest successes were against Khathban's two brigades, but luckily Hussein Rashid's 3rd Armoured Division was not seriously engaged and in the morning staged a counter-attack into the enemy's southern flank using 6th Armoured and 8th Mechanised Brigades, while Sa'adi committed 33rd Special Forces Brigade from the west. The Iranians lacked sufficient armour to contain the threat, and under heavy air attack fell back, again screened by the IRIA, losing only 500 prisoners.

This failure, on top of what the Iraqi dictator described as the 'mother of all disasters', was too great to save Khathban, who was relieved on 17 July. It is possible that 9th Armoured Division's troubles were a combination of Khathban's bungling and a flow of inexperienced commanders following the heavy losses during the last battles in Iran. On the night 17/18 July, Sa'adi visited 5th Mechanised Division headquarters and they agreed substantial reinforcements were needed and that 9th Armoured Division should be withdrawn as soon as possible.

It was clear Sa'adi lacked infantry to hold the forward line until the reinforcements arrived and, as Shukur's 6th Armoured Division had not been significantly engaged, the III Corps commander used its headquarters for a reaction force with 16th and 30th Armoured and 25th Mechanised Brigades, and 10th Independent Armoured Brigade, with the ultimate objective of retaking 9th Armoured Division's forward strongpoints. In the meantime Sa'adi successfully gambled that that 5th Mechanised Division could hold the line until he completed preparations for a set-piece counter-attack from 18 until 21 July with 3rd Armoured Division, adjusting its positions ready to launch another riposte northwards. Sa'adi and Makki then toured the divisions on 19-20 July completing their plans so that everything was ready by 21 July.

Third Offensive 21–22 July
It was just in time for that night, from 2030 hrs, the Iranians tried again to seize the initiative with 77th Division and the Pasdaran joined by part of 16th IRIA Division. Inevitably they quickly overran the forward defences and penetrated up to 10 kilometres on a 15 kilometre front, but within six hours they were again blocked by the Iraqi mechanised reserves, with heavy artillery support directed personally by the III Corps artillery chief, Major General Abdul Wahid Saeed. With dawn came the inevitable Iraqi riposte, spearheaded by 3rd Armoured Division, which slowly drove them back and claimed to have captured 39 tanks as well as 22 APCs, while Iranian dead lay scattered across the battlefield, black and bloated under the merciless sun, amid a landscape of blazing armour and installations.

Fourth Offensive 23–24 July
Their failure prompted the Iranians to make the first major revision in their plan, which meant temporarily abandoning efforts to outflank the Fish Lake north of the flooded area. To suck in the enemy reserves, and especially 3rd Armoured Division, Task Force Nasr was now ordered to break-through south of the flooded area. There all of Qadir's infantry brigades were deployed along the frontier, but he had reinforced each strongpoint with a detachment of three tanks which used ramps to help cover the obstacle zone. However, his defences followed the frontier, then swung eastwards to expose half the division to envelopment from the north.

Yet Task Force Nasr on the night of 23 to 24 July made no attempt to exploit this tactical weakness, and simply launched a frontal assault upon the four brigades (north-to-south: 109th, 49th, 45th, and 22nd) on Qadir's left. This was the most strongly fortified part of III Corps defences, yet despite the weight of artillery fire the attackers managed to struggle through the obstacle zone and up the forward slopes of the berms leading to fierce battles in the forward positions. The 45th Brigade was pushed back, exposing a bridge which carried the Basra-Khorammshahr highway, but this had been prepared for demolition and was dropped as the Pasdaran swarmed across. Then a counter-attack from the south by 22nd Infantry Brigade, together with Qadir's own armoured brigade, pushed back the Iranians who returned to their start lines having suffered heavy losses. Much of the credit for Qadir's defence was his artillery fire plan carefully prepared with General Wahid Saeed.

Fifth Offensive 28–29 July
From 25 until 27 July there was a brief lull during which the Iranian cabinet was briefed on the situation by Defence Minister Salami. Fighting was confined to artillery exchanges as well as probing in the southern sector, while roving Iraqi helicopters picked off vehicles. The brief lull gave Sa'adi time to relieve 9th Armoured Division on 27 July with 8th Infantry Division (23rd, 27th, 28th, Infantry- and 42nd Armoured Brigades) under Brigadier Diea Tawfik Ibraheem, which brought with it 12 new batteries (72 guns) and more MRLS.[26]

The losses of the 9th Armoured Division were so heavy (possibly up to 60%) that Saddam disbanded it: the salvageable elements were used to create the 17th Armoured Division in II Corps as compensation for the armour re-deployed south. By contrast both Hussein Rashid and Maher Abdul Rashid were promoted to Major General, the former during the battle for his excellent command.[27]

Even as Tawfik's troops began to occupy their new positions, Sa'adi brought him the unwelcome news that COMINT had intercepted signals indicating there would be a renewed assault on his sector and 5th Mechanised Division within 24 hours. By now the Iranians were frequently radioing *en clair* due either to a shortage of encryption machines or to the pace of the assaults meaning that encrypted communications were taking too long. Tawfik had time to insert only 42nd Armoured and 27th Infantry Brigades and assume command of 5th Mountain Brigade, before Task Force Fath began a probing attack on the night from 27 to 28 July – which alerted both the corps and its two northern divisions.

The main blow came the following night and struck the whole 5th Mechanised Division front, which had 10th and 16th Armoured Brigades holding the strongpoints on the division's right, but it was a forlorn hope as the assault was by the exhausted survivors of earlier attacks. For once there was an element of imagination in Iranian tactics with Abdul Rashid's left flank unit, 419th Brigade, struck both from the east and the north. Abdul Rashid's troops were also tired and the new assault gained ground in bitter close-quarter combat. The attack on the southern brigades, having penetrated 5 kilometres into the defences, now turned northwards in a bid to isolate all of the four forward brigades. Abdul Rashid committed his rested 15th Mechanised Brigade, joined by the newly arrived 37th Armoured and 46th Mechanised Brigades, which stabilised the situation because the 92nd Division was unable to intervene with any effect. To the south, despite having little time to prepare, the fresh 8th Division held off the enemy who made few inroads into its positions as the attacks broke down under intense artillery fire.

On the banks of the Shatt, Qadir faced a new challenge as Task Force Nasr tried in vain to reach the Fish Lake. The Pasdaran made a little progress during the night, but heavy fire restricted movement and with the dawn they hastily withdrew, and this was repeated the following evening.

On the main front, with reinforcements now arriving in strength, Sa'adi Tumma was determined to resolve the situation with a co-ordinated counter-attack again using 6th Armoured Division, which joined Abdul Rashid's armoured reserves to sweep from west to east. The attacks ground forward but paused for the night and were resumed on 31 July, by which time almost all the lost ground had been regained with the Iranians suffering further serious losses in men and material. Zahirnejhad must always have known this was a forlorn hope and as early as 29 July he visited Khomeini to give him the news that the assault had failed, and with it all hopes of a break-through.

Yet there was one last desperate attempt: after dusk of 1 August, using three widely spaced divisions reinforced with every militiaman the IRGC could find. The Iranians struck from a sliver of Iraqi territory around Zayed against 8th Infantry Division, but the attack followed the previous pattern, made few gains and was abandoned at dawn on 3 August, with Islamic fervour being sapped by the heat, humidity, exhaustion and shortage of supplies, although bloody bickering continued for a couple of days more.

The Iranians had secured an 80 square kilometre salient inside Iraq around Zayed, some 5 kilometres deep and 15 kilometres long, opposite the Fish Lake, from which they claimed they could see the lights of Basra some 25 kilometres away. This was small reward for an enterprise which had begun with such high hopes and at one time had occupied up to 300 square kilometres of Iraqi territory at high cost. US intelligence estimated the Iranians suffered 14,000 casualties (or up to 14% of the involved troops); Tehran admitted 7,000 killed, while US intelligence estimated the Iranians had also lost 250-260 AFVs.[28] They captured some 1,700 prisoners and claimed to have taken about 100 AFVs, including four T-72s, but Iraqi casualties were much lower and they had sharply reduced Iranian equipment with an estimated 20-25% loss. By 27 July the Iraqis, who dubbed the offensive 'The First Battle East of Basra', were claiming to have destroyed 339 AFVs and to have captured 59 MBTs with 22 APCs and IFVs – even though they might have lost up to 370 their own AFVs. One commentator observed: 'Operation Ramadan was, by any standard, a criminal failure of leadership and strategy', while another observed: 'The failed offensive against al-Basrah shone a spotlight on Iran's most significant military shortcomings. Iran's basic strategy was roughly equivalent to trying to use a hammer to destroy an anvil'.[29] Sayyad Shirazi would later blame 'over-confidence' following the spring successes and the Iranians certainly underestimated enemy resilience, but poor preparation and inadequate use of reconnaissance, also contributed to the failure.

The IRIA was content to allow the militia-dominated infantry to break through the defences in the hope that its mechanised forces could exploit the success, but these forces rarely seemed to seek the enemy flank or rear to envelop them. The IRIA armour was also hamstrung by inferior supply arrangements, indeed the logistical system appears to have reached near breakdown. Co-ordination between the militias and the IRIA's mechanised forces and artillery was poor, making it difficult to change fires or to exploit sudden successes. Yet the IRIA had still to master the art of logistical support for offensive operations and it lacked the flexibility to respond to major changes or crises.

The shortcomings of the IRIA were not the most serious problem for, as the IRIA leaders had tried to hint, the Pasdaran and Basiji lacked the command and control infrastructure and the heavy weapons for successful conventional operations. Their commanders often operated autonomously with little attempt to co-ordinate operations with either neighbours or support units, which led to a propensity for frontal attacks without fire support. Like many generals on the Western Front in 1915-1917, the Pasdaran commanders would prefer to reinforce forces which had been stopped or bogged down. They lacked the mobility to match the enemy mechanised reserves, as well as the training and equipment, while the shortage of radios made it difficult for commanders to recall or redirect their units, especially when they were fully engaged with enemy defences. Many Pasdaran commanders failed to time their attacks to exploit artillery support and often ignored pre-planned operational timing to rush enemy positions before artillery preparation.[30]

Here, for the first time in 18 months, the IRIA artillery was unable to dominate the battlefield. The cumulative effects of 22 months fighting were now undermining the Iranian gunners with their largely Shah-purchased US inventory of mostly self-propelled weapons such as the M109 155mm howitzer and the M107 175mm gun. Despite the diligence of Iranian purchasing commissions, supplies of ammunition and spares were running short and even before 'Ramadan' began batteries were operating at less than full strength, while compounding this problem was the fact that the irreplaceable gun barrels were literally being worn out, steadily reducing the IRIA's artillery inventory.

The offensive also proved a setback for relations between the IRIA and the Pasdaran. Combat experience from 1981 to the successful spring offensive of 1982 had seen a grudging mutual regard develop and the Pasdaran reluctantly accepted the IRIA's advice to mutual benefit. The Ghotbzadeh Plot seemed to show the regulars still harboured anti-government views, which led to more vocal criticism of the IRIA's commitment both to the war and the Islamic Revolution. The situation became so bad that during Operation 'Ramadan al-Mubarak', Zahirnejhad threatened to resign 'if unqualified people continue to meddle with the conduct of the war' and Khomeini had to order the clerics and Pasdaran to co-operate with the IRIA. The IRIA resented the fact that the Pasdaran had official favour and exerted a disproportionate weight in terms of military decision-making, although they were forced to recognize that there was a growing professionalism. This meant that in response to Pasdaran complaints about shortages of heavy weapons they were allowed to seek armour and artillery as well as creating staffs to plan, supply and administer the battle.[31]

While the Iranian SDC publicly proclaimed the offensive a success because it demonstrated the country's resolve, in reality it was profoundly disappointed not only by the defeat but also by the failure of the Iraqi Shias to rise in revolt. It was also unpleasantly surprised by the determined and tenacious resistance offered by the Iraqis who were now fighting a foreign invader themselves. Even the clerics were appalled by the scale of the Pasdaran losses and when men in the cities learned of them by word-of-mouth the numbers of volunteers were reduced to a trickle and the Pasdaran had to advertise for more. Such was their shortage of equipment that on 15 July they made a public plea for khaki uniforms, army boots and webbing. There would certainly be no swift return to the southern battlefield after so chastening an experience. The IRIA and Pasdaran were both exhausted and Zahirnejhad argued successfully for a pause to allow battered formations to receive and to train replacements as well as meditate upon the causes of their failures. Time was also needed to replace the lost armour and to expand the artillery, with the result that a lull fell on the Basra front and the Iranians spent the next 20 months licking their wounds and confining offensive activity to the northern theatres.[32]

Now it became Iran's turn to apply dogmatically a strategy that had worked well under different circumstance, only to find that it could not compensate for real disadvantages and new Iraqi resolve. Time and again the Iranians hurled themselves onto Iraqi positions with all the vigour of the past, only to shatter against well-prepared defences. The war had entered a new phase.[33]

For Saddam the thwarting of Iranian ambitions proved a huge relief which strengthened his position, boosted Iraqi morale and led the Soviet Union to abandon neutrality and re-arm the Iraqis. Some sources indicate that it was in the middle of the battle that the Iraqis began to receive maps from the United States, based upon satellite images, to identify enemy concentrations and intentions, but Iraqi sources say this was untrue. Although this and COMINT provided much useful information, intelligence collection and analysis remained a serious problem for Iraq, although there was certainly an improvement in Iraqi tactical intelligence from July 1982.[34]

US intelligence concluded that while Iraq had successfully solved the problem of defending all but the periphery of its territory through fortifications, which absorbed the enemy assault which then became vulnerable to mechanised counter-attacks, the Iranians' logistical weakness and shortage of armour prevented them driving deep into Iraq. This was probably the last time in this conflict in which ATGMs were used in large numbers for their designed role. From now onwards, at least half their targets would be static armour and strongpoints, while for every aimed missile or RPG, three or four were merely fired to harass the enemy. There also remained problems with co-ordinating the various services; the IrAAF lost a number of helicopters to the Iraqi army's own SA-7s. Henceforth, the air defence system would be closed down when they operated over the battlefield.[35]

However, the Iraqi success in Ramadan was not easily achieved, and despite the crowing statements from Baghdad Radio it was – as the Duke of Wellington said of Waterloo – 'a damn close-run thing.' The Iraqis had taken heavy losses, with at least two brigades destroyed, and the enemy retained a toe-hold, the Zayed Salient, along the border which could act as a spring-board for future assaults. This salient also compromised Saddam's desired strategy of defending the frontier and, no doubt to the relief of the more professional Iraqi officers, he was forced to accept defence in depth and abandon the old strongpoint line apart from screening forces. The berm covering the north-eastern approaches to the Fish Lake became the basis of a double strongpoint line, more strongpoints were added along the lake's western bank while within the waters was created a satanic combination of concertina wire entanglements. The Basra-Khorramshahr highway defences were strengthened, especially south of the lake, with only a screening force left along the frontier.[36]

Manning these defences would remain a problem for the Iraqi Army almost until the end of the war. The country had a smaller pool of manpower than its enemy, indeed on 22 July the Defence Ministry called up reservists born in 1953, or who were conscripted in 1972, and they were ordered to report by 3 August. The best educated or most technically skilled men were skimmed off by the air force or mechanised forces leaving few to fill the infantry battalions, and the Iraqis would begin to conscript small numbers of Arab foreigners, especially Egyptians and Sudanese, for use in support units. In April 1982, as a gesture of Arab solidarity, King Hussein of Jordan sent the 2,000-3,000 man al-Yamouk Force to join the Iraqi Army, with battalions joining 7th and 15th Infantry Divisions. Unfortunately, some of these battalions were made up of criminals who were promised a pardon in return for volunteering. Some units mutinied and while they were suppressed, the Jordanians tended to be used in secondary sectors and were withdrawn some time in 1983.[37]

Meanwhile, the Iraqis increased the inundations east of the lake until they largely covered the southern approaches. To counter this the Iranians dug a canal to drain these inundations, but its capacity to dry out the land was more than matched by the Iraqis' ability to increase the flow of water by adding a feeder channel from the Shatt. In the meantime the Fish Lake front rumbled along, with Basra now under artillery fire, despite Khomeini's injunction to avoid civilian casualties, in retaliation for Iraqi shelling of cities such as Khorramshahr and Abadan.

'Ramadan' had aimed to knock Iraq out of the war and had failed, and both sides now faced the grim prospect of a prolonged conflict.

2
BATTLES IN THE MARSHES

Despite the twin disappointments of the 'Ramadan' defeat and the absence of an Iraqi Shia rising, the SDC remained mesmerised by Basra while recognising it would be a long time before there would be sufficient armour and artillery to assault the Fish Lake line. Publicly the Iranian strategic position was explained by IRIA commander-in-chief General Shirazi: 'Our strategy is designed to liberate not only the occupied Iranian territories but also Jerusalem and all Islamic countries where people feel the need to vanquish tyranny. Ours is a war that we are waging for God and he will guide us to victory'.[1]

The frontier between Ahwaz and Khorammshahr became a huge staging area with camps, supply dumps and training grounds as the

Cheerful Pasdaran forming up at one of the embarkation points, from which they were deployed into the attack aboard a miscellany of speedboats, at the beginning of Khyber. IRGC troops sent into the battles of 1984 were better equipped than ever before, all wearing uniforms and even steel helmets. (Tom Cooper Collection)

A group of youthful Pasdaran waiting for their turn to attack through the Hoveyzeh Marshes in February 1983. (Tom Cooper Collection)

Members of at least two of many IRGC RPG-7-teams embarking an assault launch in preparation for crossing the Hoveyzeh Marshes. Notable are the characteristic rucksacks with pouches for spare rounds carried by nearly all of them. (Tom Cooper Collection)

Iranians tried to exploit operational experience in improved training. While Basra remained beyond Tehran's reach the leadership had no intention of relinquishing the strategic level (army group and above) initiative so they sought a decision on the northern and central fronts with the Valfajr (or 'Wal Fajr') series of offensives. These gained a little ground at great cost, but at the tactical level (operations within army corps) they improved the lightly armed Pasdarans' professional capabilities especially within rough terrain. In fact the Kurdish-dominated northern front with its mountain chains made a breakthrough impossible, while the deserts west of Khuzestan remained a death-trap, but as activity on the Kurdish front declined during late 1983 there was increased interest in resuming an offensive against Basra – possibly to draw reserves away from that front.[2]

The Valfajr series of operations suggested to Rezai and Safavi that it might be possible to cross the Hawizah Marshes and take Basra from the north. They began to canvas support for this idea during 1983, with the bonus from the clerics' viewpoint, that the terrain favoured Pasdaran troops rather than the IRIA. The marsh was largely impassable for AFVs, it was lightly held and the defences around it were weak so Tehran could conceal the assembly of a Pasdaran-based assault force intended to strike southwards to outflank the northern Fish Lake defences, and then push down to Basra. To reduce the threat from the IrAF and IrAAC it was decided to launch the offensive during the tail end of the rainy season when an average of 28.5mm of rain falls in January, and drops to 15.2 mm in February. The low clouds would restrict enemy air power but the water levels within the marsh would be high enough to permit rapid movement by boat.

The Iranians, who had now learned the virtue of planning and preparation, created a network of roads along the border, and especially in the south, during the summer of 1983 which they used

While most of about 500 assault boats used by the IRGC for crossing the Hoveyzeh Marshes were unarmed, some had a heavy machinegun installed for air defence purposes. This one has a 14.5mm KPV-1. (Tom Cooper Collection)

In addition to hundreds of minor boats, the IRGC made use of larger barges for crossing the Hoveyzeh Marshes too. This one is hauling a cargo of water or petrol to the frontlines. (Tom Cooper Collection)

Despite many reports to the contrary (especially in the West), the Iranians paid great attention to CASEVAC and MEDEVAC. This boat was photographed while evacuating at least two injured Pasdaran. Usually, these would be brought to one of the many field hospitals positioned close to the embarkation points. (Tom Cooper Collection)

to fill supply dumps. To prevent the enemy inundating the marshes from the Tigris, during 1983 the Iranians began to dig a 58 kilometre-long canal from the River Karun to drain away flood waters and this was completed by early 1984. In response Iraq created a new set of large embankments which ran parallel to the front. Meanwhile, the Iranian forces began to train and to equip their forces for assaults across rivers and obstacles as well as positioning forces to bypass them. The region was selected because the defenders' weakness was shown by the lack of military activity, apart from the occasional clash of patrols, and an attack on several axes would force the enemy to scatter his forces and prevent them from using large numbers of AFVs. The mosquito-ridden Hawizah Marshes would be the focus of bitter fighting over the next 12 months, and at the time of the Iran-Iraq War they were a formidable obstacle to conventional armies especially during the rainy season. Inhabited by the so-called Marsh Arabs (Ma'dan), the Hawizah Marshes were fed from the Tigris (Nahr Dijlah) by the Rivers Musharah and al-Zahla from the north and while their boundaries are fluid, they are generally about 50 kilometres from north to south and 65-105 kilometres from east to west, and cover an area of some 3,000 square kilometres, although this can expand during the rainy season to 60 and 115 kilometres respectively.[3]

The northern and central parts were permanently flooded to a depth of up to 6 metres, with open stretches of water bounded by dense reed beds up to 7 metres above the water level, and which can conceal movement. There were three small lakes in this part, the largest being the Hawr al Hawizah and Hawr Limar Sawan, and there were two areas of firm land. Most of the Ma'dan lived in this region in tiny villages of houses made of reeds on a reed-woven base, anchored to the sand and the silt beneath the water, or on tiny islets which were little more than muddy embankments. Some villages were linked by narrow (5-metre) embankments or 'bunds', a few metres above the water level, or by a few narrow, navigable channels, but most of the channels were clogged with reeds or weeds.

West of the marshes lay the meandering Tigris which is 75-250 metres wide and can flood the surrounding plain to a depth of 3 metres. At what would be the northern end of the battlefield was a broad strip of land some 10 kilometres wide between the river and the marshes, just north of al-Uzayr (also al-Azair, as-Sulayb and Ozair). From here a finger of land some 4-5 kilometres broad and 5 kilometres long pointed north-east into the marshes, with the village of al-Harrah at its tip. From Harrah a narrow road ran along a bund through the villages al-Beida (also al-Bayda, El Bauda and Beizeh) and Madina back to Uzayr where there was a bridge across the Tigris to the Baghdad-Basra highway which came south from al-Amarah. This highway, with the Baghdad-Basra railway some 15 kilometres to the west, ran for 40 kilometres alongside the western bank of the Tigris to al-Qurnah, where the two rivers meet to form the Shatt, while from the river's eastern bank was a narrow strip of raised land averaging 5-6 kilometres wide to the marsh edge.

An Iranian tank-transporter seen while carrying a British-made 55-tonne BH.7 Wellington air-cushion landing craft towards the Hoveyzeh Marshes in preparation for Operation Khaiber. (Tom Cooper Collection)

The southern part of the marshes was more seasonal in nature, with the deepest channels only 3 metres deep, and here significant attempts began to drain the marsh. In the 1970s, the British oil company BP led a boycott of Iraq after it nationalised foreign oil producers, but in June 1972 the Latin American producer Petrobras Braspetro of Brazil (Petrobras or Braspetro) broke the embargo. A grateful Baghdad gave Petrobras concessions to discover and to exploit oil on behalf of the Iraqi National Oil Corporation, and during the 1970s Brazilian prospectors discovered that an extension of the Great Rumaila Triangle oil field lay under the marshes, with a potential 7 billion barrels of heavy-to-medium oil.[4]

To exploit this wealth Petrobras began draining water from the south-eastern corner of the marshes and excavating sand and mud to create causeways, dikes and canals, together with an embankment-bounded island totalling 170 square kilometres. Split by a 2-kilometre lateral drainage channel into two areas dubbed the Majnoon (Crazy) Islands (Jazaer-e Majmun also written Majnun), dotted with oil rigs and with a small administrative centre in the south-western corner of South Majnoon.

By the time Iraq invaded Iran, Petrobras had reached the engineering phase for production facilities and had 14 drilling rigs at both Majnoon and at the nearby Nahr Umr field, while there were

The Islamic Republic of Iran Navy (IRIN) deployed six of its Wellington hovercraft for Khyber. Powered by a Rolls-Royce Proteus Gnome gas turbine, these could carry up to 60 men or 18 tonnes at speeds up to 60 knots. (Tom Cooper Collection)

more than 20 exploration wells in Majnoon, one of which had penetrated 14 oil-bearing zones. When the war broke out Petrobras' foreign oil workers fled after capping the wells.[5]

West of the Majnoons, between the marshes and the Tigris, lay a 5-7 kilometre-wide strip of intensely-cultivated farmland which ran 15 kilometres down to Tuyrabah and featured numerous irrigation channels and palm groves. The key Baghdad-Basra highway runs west of the Tigris and the meanderings of the river mean it often runs along its bank before reaching Qurnah, which is bounded in the east by the Tigris and in the south by Euphrates (al-Furat). The highway crosses the latter river on two bridges before running to Basra but, in this battlefield, it is linked to the west by only two bridges, at Uzayr and Nashwah (Nashveh in Farsi), the latter 25 kilometres north of Basra. On the opposite bank a smaller, gravelled, road ran along an embankment which ran parallel to the highway to Basra.

The Majnoons lay only 2 kilometres from where the international

Prior to Operation Khyber, the IRGC took over a number of stored BTR-50s from the IRIA, re-engined them with US-made diesels and deployed them in combat to make use of their amphibious capabilities – as 'Kashayar'. Two of these can be seen towing a section of a pontoon bridge through the Hoveyzeh Marshes. (Tom Cooper Collection)

For moving heavier equipment as well as troops and supplies through the Hoveyzeh, the Iranians acquired pressurised Styrofoam floats from South Korea, which were then used as the basis for pontoon bridges. The longest of these was over 30 kilometres long. (Tom Cooper Collection)

frontier turned north from the 31st Parallel, which meant they were within easy reach if the Iranians wanted a base to strike south and this was the basis on which Operation Khyber was prepared from early in 1984. The decision to change offensive activity away from conventional trials of strength allowed the SDC to slowly build up the Islamic Republic's forces so that the IRIA had some 300,000 men while the Pasdaran had a similar figure which could be augmented temporarily by up to 100,000 Basiji. An artillery park of some 600-1,000 guns had been assembled although, compared with the start of the war, its battlefield mobility was restricted because it was easier to acquire towed, than self-propelled, ordnance. The armoured force had also been expanded through a combination of 'heroic' maintenance and cannibalisation work on American and British vehicles augmented by the acquisition of Chinese and former Iraqi vehicles to give the IRIA 500 MBTs and the Pasdaran 250, most distributed to independent tank battalions.[6]

The Spearhead
This campaign would mark a stage in the war when operations would be dominated by the clerics' forces; the Pasdaran and the Basiji. The Pasdaran had grown from a fervent, but untrained, police-force-cum-militia into a counter-insurgency force and then into a semi-conventional army which was becoming increasingly professional, with uniforms and saluting, although leaders were given no formal rank and everyone was addressed as 'Brother'. The provincial platoons had gradually coalesced into battalions, the battalions grouped into brigades, whose support was strengthened, and the brigades into divisions. The Pasdaran had now also created artillery, armoured and mechanised units manned by the more experienced, or better educated, troops, although it was not until September 1985 that it would be formally divided into specialist branches.[7]

Each brigade had four infantry battalions of 300-325 men, now augmented by a reconnaissance company and a support company with heavy machineguns, 81mm mortars and recoilless artillery, together with a logistics unit to total some 1,400 men. There were three brigades in a division which also had a support battalion with 107mm MRLS, 81-120mm mortars, recoilless artillery and air-defence weapons, together with reconnaissance and engineer battalions, while increasingly they received an artillery battalion

An abandoned Iraqi artillery position; originally constructed to cover the marshes. Like so many forward positions, it proved vulnerable to infiltration and attacks by the IRGC's infantry using speedboats. (Tom Cooper Collection)

of radios meant the IRIA received the lion's share of communication equipment and this severely restricted Pasdaran command and control which often depended upon vulnerable land lines or even more vulnerable messengers. This would be a serious problem when the tiny divisional staffs were 'double-hatted' to become task force commands.

The Pasdaran were usually 18-26 year-old volunteers, unmarried, and largely drawn from the urban poor with selection often based upon the family, or personal, relationships with the clerics. This relationship spurred recruitment together with the desire for social change and patriotism to give the Pasdaran a sense of purpose reinforced by good pay and benefits. Officially all were committed to the ideals of the Islamic Revolution but while most were fiercely patriotic the degree to which they imbibed the Shia fascination for martyrdom varied from man to man. The Pasdaran were certainly run by zealous commanders who led from the front and expected revolutionary fervour to achieve victory. The downside upon unit cohesion was heavy casualties due to command and control weaknesses. These heavy casualties meant experienced men were replaced by raw recruits who diluted unit effectiveness. Even the Pasdaran were not immune to the demoralising psychological effects of heavy casualties and gradually the flow of volunteers slowed to a trickle forcing the provinces increasingly to despatch conscripts, many of whom were less driven by religious rhetoric.[8]

Increasingly the Pasdaran faced a nominally fixed period of service of 24 months, contrasting with 30 months for the IRIA, but in both services the men could re-enlist. Units were normally kept in camps and deployed for short, intense, periods of combat before being withdrawn to unwind; chatting, pursuing hobbies and playing sport such as volleyball and soccer. This certainly helped reduce the toll from battle fatigue and after unwinding they could return to training, but the heavy losses of veterans meant many units returned to action with a growing ratio of raw recruits who, in turn, suffered heavy losses to steadily erode unit combat effectiveness. However, a major health problem, especially for troops who were not native to

with 105mm-130mm guns and some 122mm MRLS, to give them up to 6,500 men.

While the Pasdaran had learned from working alongside the IRIA, the small command teams had little experience of staff work, while the logistical organisation remained rudimentary. With each of the 11 Pasdaran regions jealously guarding its independence from the Pasdaran Ministry in Tehran, it was impossible to co-ordinate a constant flow of supplies and replacements to the front, although the ministry controlled the supply of weapons and ammunition. Formations appear to have organised the distribution of supplies to front-line units using daring drivers in civilian pick-up trucks or even motorcyclists whose forays around the Forward Edge of Battle (FEBA) exposed them to enemy fire. The Iranians' perennial lack

To protect their troops from Iraqi aircraft and helicopters during Operation Khyber, the Iranians organized an air defence system consisting of early warning radars, MIM-23B I-HAWK SAMs, a wide variety of anti-aircraft artillery and 9K32 Strela-2 (or SA-7 Grail) man-portable missile systems (MANPADS). This Pasdaran is posing with his Strela launcher: the weapon fired a 9.8kg infra-red homing missile, with a 1.15kg warhead, out to a range of 3,700 metres. (Tom Cooper Collection)

the western desert region, was Sand Fly Fever, a debilitating disease whose symptoms included not only severe fever but also headaches, aching limbs and light sensitivity. Both the Naples and Sicilian strains of the virus were encountered by Iranian medical staff, although almost all the troops had the latter strain which needed treatment with bed rest, pain medication and fluids for a problem also encountered by Iraqi Army doctors.[9]

The Basiji, by contrast, were the poorly-trained cannon-fodder of the Islamic Revolution grouped into company-sized, mosque-based, units of up to 200 men designated 'battalions', two or three of which would be attached to each Pasdaran brigade They tended to be older than the Pasdaran, generally aged 20-30 although their ages ranged from 13-70, often married, uneducated and usually they came from the rural poor. Khomeini opened the Iranian New Year in 1982 (20 March) by allowing boys of 12-18 to join the Basij, their enlistment documents being dubbed 'Passports to Paradise'. After Khyber the Pasdaran Ministry would claim that 57% of the assault force (i.e. some 80,000 troops) were 'school children,' but the term probably ranges from schoolboy Basiji to teenage Pasdaran. Like the Pasdaran the ideals of the Islamic Revolution motivated Basiji recruitment. The sense of community provided unit cohesion, like the British Pals Battalions of the First World War, but it also meant that heavy casualties would have a devastating impact upon their home villages and towns.[10]

Every piece of dry land in Hoveyzeh was used for deployment of heavier equipment. This islet was occupied by a 23mm ZU-23 anti-aircraft cannon, operated by the IRGC. This weapon had a high rate of fire and a range of about 2,000 metres. As such, it proved too short-ranged for effective use even against Iraqi helicopter gunships. Nevertheless, it proved effective against infantry and even lightly armoured vehicles. (Tom Cooper Collection)

Their rural background meant that Basiji mobilisation was restricted to the periods between sowing and harvest and they rarely served for more than three months. They would be transported from their mosques piecemeal to assembly camps, usually sleeping on the bare earth because no tents were provided, which made it difficult for any intelligence agency to monitor build ups. Often they took their own food and water, which mosques would replenish when possible, and at the front might they would receive a weapon and a little ammunition, often a single magazine, then a fortnight's military training. Their fervour would be sustained by fiery speeches, readings from the Koran, hymns and prayers from their religious leaders before they attacked.

The Basiji, like most militias, were little more than a wild mob with little or no command and control, who would simply charge forward, sometimes accidentally clearing minefields with their own bodies because they were unaware of the mines' presence, then kept going out of sheer terror. Contrary to numerous accounts during and

A Bell 214A of the IRIAA seen while disembarking commandos of the 23rd Special Forces Brigade during a mission behind enemy lines in Hoveyzeh. (Tom Cooper Collection)

after the war of Pasdaran 'human wave' attacks, their tactics were far more sophisticated. The Pasdaran would carefully reconnoitre enemy defences to determine their weaknesses and use the Basiji to help clear the approaches. They would then infiltrate the defences, overwhelming positions were possible and isolating the strongest positions whose defenders would then be subdued by small arms fire before they were stormed.

Planning for Operation Khyber

The operation was reportedly planned by Major General Hassan Abshenasan and although it was to be commanded by Deputy Ground Forces Commander General Ali Jalali. For the first time SFOH (Karbala Command) was not in sole control as the spearhead was exclusively under the Pasdaran Najaf Command. Contrary to many reports, efforts of interservice co-operation and mutually supporting joint operations were at the heart of this operation, for while the Pasdaran would provide most of the spearhead, all the traditional services provided support in terms of fire power, logistics, air and even maritime power. The militias had nine divisions and seven infantry brigades, together with an armoured brigade, a total of some 95,000 Pasdaran and Basiji, but only one artillery battalion per division, totalling some 115 guns (except for the Task Force 'Honain' division which commanded no batteries). By contrast the 35,000 IRIA personnel, in five brigades, were supported by some 200 guns, although many batteries would also support the Pasdaran.[11]

As well as nearly 100 lighter helicopters, the IRIAA and the IRIAF deployed their CH-47C Chinooks for hauling light artillery pieces and vehicles to the frontlines. This example was photographed while carrying a jeep with a 106mm recoilless gun. At least one of the Chinooks involved survived a hit from an Iraqi interceptor that disabled the rear engine. (Tom Cooper Collection)

A Bell 214A Esfahan of the IRIAA seen while navigating low over the Hoveyzeh Marshes. Some of the Iranian assaults involved up to 40 such helicopters. (Tom Cooper Collection)

Khybers' objective was to isolate the Iraqi forces around Basra to pave the way for their destruction and the city's capture, but 'Ramadan al-Mubarak' clearly demonstrated this could not be achieved in one move. Instead it would be conducted in two phases; the first to secure what the US Army describes as 'the line of departure' or 'jump-off point' from which the isolation of the enemy could then be achieved.[12]

Najaf Command was to secure bridgeheads on the western and southern edges of the marshes with Pasdaran forces augmented by 1st Battalion of the 23rd Special Forces Brigade and a battalion of the 55th Airborne Brigade. Two task forces with some 15,000 men would secure the right flank; Nasr in the north would take the firm ground north of Uzayr with 5th Nasr Division and 15th Imam Hassan Brigades, then take the bridge across the Tigris at Uzayr to cut the Baghdad-Basra highway; while to the south Task Force Hadid with 21st Imam Reza and 44th Qamar Bani Hashem Brigades would secure the eastern Tigris including the cultivated area to threaten Qurnah in the southwest.

The main strike forces were Task Forces Honain and Badr which would enter the marshes from the east then swing southwards. The former, with the 27th Mohamad Rasoolallah Division together with

An Iranian M47M drives over the Khyber Bridge to North Majnoon Islet. Notable are a few branches placed on each pontoon in the vain attempt to camouflage from air attacks: they were certainly more effective in concealing this huge construction from view from the ground. (Tom Cooper Collection)

18th Al-Ghadir and 33rd Al-Mahdi Brigades (11,000 men) would first take North Majnoon Island then reinforce Badr, which had 17th Ali Ibn Abu-Taleb and 41st Sarallah Divisions, with 10th Seyed ol-Shohada Brigade (19,000 men). They were to first take South Majnoon, then push past Qurnah to take Nashwah. Once the Majnoons were taken then the IRIA 1st Area Support Command would establish a reliable supply route eastwards to their main supply base of Talaiyeh (also Taialyeh).

When these forces were in place two more task forces would drive some 60 kilometres westwards to Nashwah under separate commands; Najaf and the Army's Karbala Command. Najaf's Task Force Fath, with 21,000 men, was to strike from Talaiyeh towards Nashwah with 8th Najaf Ashraf, 19th Fajr and 31st Ashura Divisions, but it needed the expertise of the IRIA's Task Force Zeid with 31,000 men and some 250 MBTs to punch a hole through the

Table 4: IRIA/IRGC, Southern Forward Operations HQ (Karbala HQ), February 1984

Corps	Division & HQ	Brigades & Notes
	Direct Combat Support Group (IRIAA)	2 attack battalions (AH-1Js), 3 assault battalions (Bell 214As), 2 reconnaissance battalions (Bell 206), 2 transport battalions (CH-47C)
Task Force Najaf		23rd SF Brigade (1st Battalion only)
		55th Airborne Brigade (1 battalion only)
Task Force Nasr	5th Nasr Infantry Division (IRGC)	
		15th Imam Hassan Infantry Brigade (IRGC)
Task Force Hadid		21st Imam Reza Infantry Brigade (IRGC)
		44th Qamar Bani Hashem Infantry Brigade (IRGC)
Task Force Honain	27th Mohammad Rasoolallah Infantry Division (IRGC)	including 18th al-Ghadir and 33rd al-Mahdi Infantry Brigades
Task Force Badr	17th Ali Ibn Abu Talib Infantry Division (IRGC)	
	41st Sarallah Infantry Division (IRGC)	
		10th Seyed ol-Shohada Infantry Brigade (IRGC)
Task Force Fath	8th Najaf Ashraf Infantry Division (IRGC)	
	19th Fajr Infantry Division (IRGC)	
	31st Ashura Infantry Division (IRGC)	
Task Force Zeid	16th Armoured Division	1 brigade only
	92nd Armoured Division	1 brigade only
	21st Infantry Division (IRIA)	1 brigade only
	28th Infantry Division (IRIA)	1 brigade only
	77th Infantry Division (IRIA)	1 brigade only
		20th Ramadan Armoured Brigade (IRGC)
		72nd Moharram Armoured Brigade (IRGC)
	7th Valli Assr Infantry Division (IRGC)	
	14th Imam Hussein Infantry Division (IRGC)	
		28th Zafar Infantry Brigade (IRGC)

Table 5: III and IV Corps Iraqi Army, February 1984

Corps	Division	Brigades & Notes
III Corps	Corps Troops	8th Border Brigade; 33rd SF Brigade; 65th Commando Brigade; III Corps Artillery Brigade (10 artillery and 5 MRLS batteries)
	4th Mountain Division	5th Mountain Brigade; 18th and 29th Infantry Brigades
	5th Mechanised Division	26th and 55th Armoured Brigades; 15th and 20th Mechanised Brigades; 19th and 419th Infantry Brigades
	8th Infantry Division	22nd, 23rd, 28th, 425th Infantry Brigades
IV Corps	Corps Troops	66th and 68th Commando Brigades; IV Corps Artillery Brigade
	10th Armoured Division	17th and 42nd Armoured Brigades; 24th Mechanised Brigade
	14th Infantry Division	18th and 422nd Infantry Brigades
	19th Infantry Division	108th, 113th, 419th Infantry Brigades
Reserve Forces	3rd Armoured Division	6th and 12th Armoured Brigades; 8th Mechanized Brigade
	6th Armoured Division	16th, 30th and 56th Armoured Brigades; 25th Mechanised Brigade

northern defensive belt to reach Nashwah. Supported by the 33rd and 55th Artillery Groups, it was based upon a brigade each of the 16th and 92nd IRIA Armoured Divisions, and the 21st, 28th and 77th Infantry Divisions reinforced by the Pasdaran's 20th Ramadan and 72nd Moharram Armoured Brigades, the 7th Vali Asr and 14th Imam Hossein Divisions as well as the 28th Zafar Brigade. The IRIA had a secondary role in this offensive, but it continued to provide considerable expertise in planning and logistics as well as providing artillery and engineering support. Much of the 1st Area Support Command was assembled, with bulldozers ready to push roads from Talaiyeh into the marshes and augment these roads with pontoon and other bridging equipment, while light pontoon bridges were made from Korean-supplied Styrofoam floats with planking laid down on them to augment bunds and help move infantry and light supplies through the wetlands. The IRIAA would provide some 130 aircraft under the personal command of Lieutenant Colonel Mohamad-Hossein Jajali, who would fly the first night mission of the offensive. Forward resupply points were established so the IRIAA could bring ammunition to the task forces moving through the marshes

A rare photograph of an Iranian M48A5 from the 16th Armoured Division. A mechanized brigade from this unit was deployed on the southern edge of the marshes for Operation Khyber. (Tom Cooper Collection)

Medical personnel scrambling to evacuate casualties and orderlies from one of the CH-47Cs of the IRIAF (serial 5-4075), deployed in support of ground forces during Operation Khyber. (Tom Cooper Collection)

The 106mm M40 recoilless gun was another primary means of providing direct fire support to Iranian troops advancing through the Hoveyzeh Marshes. The gunners on the left of this pair have just fired, causing a typical trace of smoke to drift away. (Tom Cooper Collection)

M38A1 jeeps and different variants of Toyota 4WDs mounting BGM-71 TOW ATGMs proved potent direct-fire-support systems, somewhat balancing Iraqi advantages in armour. Although un-armoured, they proved capable of facing even the best-protected of Iraqi MBTs because of their ability to engage from stand-off ranges. (Tom Cooper Collection)

with a dozen helicopters, half of them large Chinook transports each capable of carrying 33 men or 8.5 tonnes of cargo, assigned to Task Force Badr.[13]

The Islamic Republic of Iran Navy (IRIN) would also play an important role and established a command to support the seizure of the Majnoon Islands. This included the Hovercraft Brigade whose six BH-7 could each move 60 men or 18 tonnes and a base with some 500 boats and barges which varied 'from large aluminium ones, capable of carrying up to 100 men, to small craft with outboard motors, able only to take half-a-dozen or so'.

There were also barges capable of carrying APCs and the watercraft would also be used to evacuate the wounded.[14]

Unlike 'Ramadan al-Mubarak,' the operation would be fought in relatively cooler times, the temperature averaging 68-76°F (20-24°C) and there was certainly no threat from heat exhaustion or dehydration. There was, however, extensive reconnaissance by the IRIAF, Iranian Special Forces from 23rd Brigade and Pasdaran scouting units, aided by Marsh Arab sympathisers, some of them members of Hakim's Badr Brigades. These helped to identify weak points in the defence and the fact that much of it was in the hands of the Popular Army, the Ba'ath Party militia.

Iraqi preparations

In early February the Iraqis reviewed contingency plans to meet anticipated threats. Within each corps sector at least three infantry or Special Forces (Alwiyat al-Quwat al-Khassah)/Commando (Alwiyat al-Maqhaweer) brigades were allocated a reaction role, together with armoured/mechanised divisions. The IV Corps (Major General Thabit Sultan) defending Maysan Province in the north and III Corps defending Basra Province in the south were no exceptions. Both corps were under new commanders; Sultan had relieved Major General Husham Sabbah al-Fakhri at the beginning of the year when Fakhri became Deputy Chief-of-Staff for Operations. In January 1984 Lieutenant General Maher Abdul Rashid assumed command of III Corps after previously leading I Corps and 5th Mechanised Division. He came from Tikrit, was a relative of Saddam, and his daughter would later marry Uday Hussein. While generally regarded as a competent commander he was foul-mouthed and regarded as 'a very nasty person.'[15]

The Iranian offensive would strike along the corps' mutual boundary at a time when Sultan and Rashid were focused upon threats from the east to Amarah and Basra respectively and their forces were spread thinly to cover the 150 kilometres between them. Sultan had 14th Infantry Division on his right with 18th and 422nd Infantry Brigades holding the sector from Uzayr northwards, but was deployed to cover the Baghdad-Basra highway with some 6,000 men. To screen the marshes, where there seemed only a minor threat from raiders and infiltrators supporting Shia insurgents, the Iraqis deployed 8th Border Guard Brigade and some sailors. As early as May 1981 the Iraqis had considered draining the marshes and planned a 12-metre-wide levee some 3.5 metres above the water linked to similar levees built around Basra, but the plan was never implemented. Border Guards and boat-operating sailors occupied a few marsh-side villages from which boat patrols were despatched, but most of its 1,500 men held a line of fortified police stations along the main route down the eastern bank of the Tigris. To deal with any serious incursions Sultan had in reserve 10th Armoured Division (with 17th Armoured and 24th Mechanised Brigades) while 42nd Armoured Brigade was a permanent reaction force north of the marshes together with the newly formed 66th and 68th Commando Brigades; some 15,700 men with 300 MBTs.[16]

Rashid also kept his regulars out of the marshes whose southwestern corner was covered by 19th Infantry Division (108th, 113th, 419th Infantry Brigades) which screened Qurnah. The apparent lack of threat meant the Iraqis made no attempt to fortify this line, but rather relied upon a screen of forward posts which patrolled the marsh edges while the bulk of the division was held back as a reaction force. Within the marshes was a Popular Army sector of three battalions, probably augmented by Border Guards, who were responsible for the security of the Majnoon Islands, and some naval personnel operating patrol boats; and these brought the number of III Corps defenders to about 15,000 men.[17]

The bulk of III Corps remained in, or behind, the Fish Lake

defences which had been substantially expanded since 'Ramadan' had demonstrated the futility of trying to make the frontier the main line of resistance (MLR), and on 16 February the importance of the new defences was again stressed. The angle of battalion strongpoints covering the north-eastern approaches to the Fish Lake had been strengthened to provide both security and greater economy of forces. Holding these defences were the 4th Mountain Infantry Division in the north and 8th Infantry Division and the 5th Mechanised Division in the east. In reserve were 3rd and 6th Armoured Divisions, 33rd Special Forces and 65th Commando Brigades, and they would be supported by III Corps artillery with 10 tube and five MRLS batteries; a grand total of some 90,000 men with 675 MBTs. In addition Basra Command had 95th Infantry Brigade which could also be deployed. While COMINT alerted the Iraqi leadership that something was happening around the marshes most probably agreed with the III Corps chief of staff General Makki, that 'it never crossed my mind that they would cross in that area'. For the Iraqis the Pasdarans' flexible chain of command and logistics arrangements continued to make it difficult for them to determine the enemy plan and later they would begin to conclude, wrongly, there were no chains of command among the militias.[18]

Most of the Iraqi positions in the Hoveyzeh Marshes looked like this: sand-bagged, or even concrete, machinegun nests. One such reinforced position was usually constructed at each of the corners of Iraqi triangular strongpoints, surrounded by 3-metres high berms. (Albert Grandolini Collection)

Khyber begins

The offensive began on 14 February with Task Force Zeid staging a week-long series of diversionary attacks just across the border north-east of Khorammshahr. Sometimes supported by helicopters, these diversions, together with raids and bombardments, were designed to confuse the Iraqi leadership as to the main axes of the offensive and appear to have succeeded.

Following the code words 'Ya Rasulollah' the first phase of Khyber began on the evening of 22 to 23 February as Task Force Nasr began moving across the marshes for a sub-offensive, reportedly called 'Fatima al Zahra'. Its two brigades moved along the bunds, sometimes using motorcycles or by boat along the channels, while heliborne commandos struck enemy artillery positions. One bund ran to Beida, at the tip of a sandy peninsula with Sakhra (Sabkha or Sakhrah) some 1.5 kilometres to the south, and then Ajairda (Ajrada or Agirda) where there was a bridge across the Tigris, which was to be seized to provide a bridgehead near the Baghdad-Basra highway.[19]

Heavily camouflaged Iraqi troops in position on the western banks of the Hoveyzeh Marshes. The soldier in the foreground is armed with an RPG-7. (Albert Grandolini Collection)

The spearhead arrived at Beida during the night by boat and seized the undefended village, then began moving westwards to take Sakhra. Inevitably, the attack lost momentum because the boats which had brought in the assault force had to return to pick up reinforcements and supplies, but by dawn the spearhead was close to the river and had taken Ajairda to establish a small bridgehead. Although surprised by the strength of the attack, Sultan reacted quickly and despite the loss of some batteries he was able to bring down heavy

An Iraqi ZPU-4 14.5mm KVP heavy machinegun, positioned to protect the road along the Tigris River. Each ZPU-4 had a 40-round ammunition container and could fire 600 rounds a minute out to a range of 3,000 metres. (Albert Grandolini Collection)

MIDDLE EAST@WAR VOLUME 24

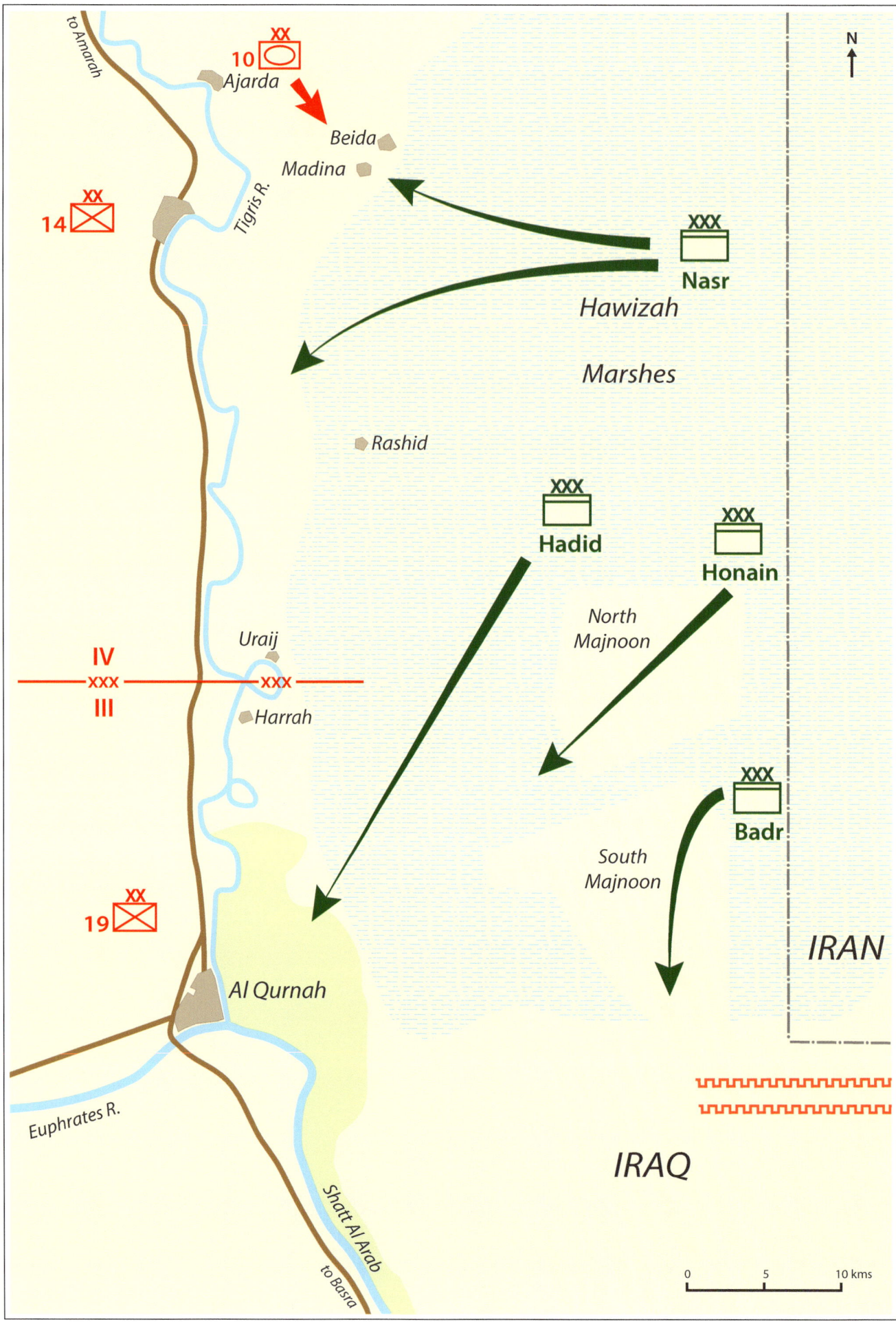

Map 2: Operation Khyber: Opening stages

artillery fire upon the bridgehead, although many shells exploded into the marshes which absorbed much of the blast and fragments. The Pasdaran used camouflage to blend in with the terrain, but while successful against high performance combat aircraft it was of little use against helicopters, especially the 'Hinds'.

The Border Guards reportedly fought as well as the Army's troops although this was claimed to be '...with bravery born of despair...'.[20] Meanwhile helicopters brought in IRIA airborne troops and reinforcements to key areas allowing them to seal the end of the peninsula. Meanwhile, Iraqi air power interdicted the waterways, flying 94 fixed- and 135 rotary-wing sorties during the day, to restrict the flow of men and materials, especially anti-armour weapons, to the bridgehead. This had little effect and the absence of Iraqi Forward Air Controllers (FAC) meant there was little Close Air Support (CAS) but the IRIAF -restricted to no more than 100 sorties by the need to conserve its remaining assets – attempted to interdict IV Corps' convoys driving south. A few sorties temporarily disrupted Sultan's efforts to support his neighbour, but bad weather meant most were ineffective.

But the attackers were in a trap of their own making, scattered along an exposed sandbank and unable to dig deep due to the high water table. Elsewhere along the bank the Pasdaran continued to probe and push, sometimes mortaring the highway. Popular Army units were hastily mobilised to secure the Baghdad-Basra highway and Uzayr, until the arrival of 10th Armoured Division's 24th Mechanised Brigade, which Sultan swiftly brought south, while its 17th Armoured Brigade swept down the eastern bank of the Tigris – together with 68th Commando Brigade – on a rainy 25 February. The threat along the weak boundary of both corps led Saddam to authorise the creation on 26 February of a new command, East of Tigris Operations Headquarters (ETOH) under Fakhri, who was familiar with the sector and who established his headquarters at Uzayr within seven hours. In addition to 10th Armoured Division he was assigned Sultan's 14th Infantry Division and 18th Infantry Division (95th, 702nd, and 704th Infantry Brigades) while the newly formed 66th Commando Brigade was flown to Uzayr from its training camp, as Fakhri was ordered to end minor operations and prepare for a set-piece counter-offensive.[21]

On 27 February Fakhri launched his counter-offensive, Operation 'al-Wajib al-Muqaddas' ('Holy or Sacred Mission') under 10th Armoured Division command, towards Beida. A direct attack was launched by 24th Mechanised and 66th Commando Brigades from Uzayr, while 17th Armoured Brigade with 68th Commando Brigade made a flank attack towards Sakhra. It was heralded in the early hours by a spectacular success for the IrAF whose fighters detected and attacked 50 helicopters carrying a battalion to the Majnoons and claimed eight of them.[22]

With strong air support – the Iraqis flew 247 fixed-wing and 203 rotary-wing sorties that day – the Iraqi AFVs drove down the narrow bunds, braving RPG fire to crush the infantry in their fox holes,

This battered Iraqi T-54 or T-55 was deployed in support of the III Corps' counter-attack from the south – before it was captured by Pasdaran and turned against its former owners. (Tom Cooper Collection)

Loaded with ammunition boxes and food on the rear deck, this BTR-50 was probably used to resupply forward-deployed Iraqi troops. Notable is the observation tower in the background: because the Hoveyzeh Marshes were flat and devoid of any major features, any observation position represented an important piece of real estate. (Tom Cooper Collection)

Operation Khyber cost the Iranians up to 60,000 casualties. Here a line of Pasdaran captured by the troops of the Iraqi III Corps are paraded for the cameras, their hands tied. (Albert Grandolini Collection)

with Sakhra falling on the first day and Beida on 28 February. Yet this was no walk-over, and Sultan would later describe the fighting as some of the fiercest he had encountered, with much hand-to-hand fighting. The Pasdaran broke and fled into the marsh, where many were drowned and some electrocuted because Fakhri had placed electrodes in some channels. Helicopters claimed others, as well as 39 boats, and later 3,000 Iranian dead were buried in a bulldozed mass grave. Fakhri continued sweeping along the east bank of the Tigris from 29 February towards Ajairda with 17th Armoured Brigade with 68th Commando Brigade advanced south while 24th Mechanised Brigade and 66th Commando Brigade moved north from Uzayr to retake Ajairda with strong artillery and helicopter support, then pushed the enemy into the marsh.

A feature of this operation was the first major use of poison gas by the Iraqis – apparently mustard gas – largely against communications, although Fakhri denied their use on 5 March. The Iranians reported 400 chemical casualties by 28 February from agents delivered two days earlier, a figure which soon expanded to 1,100, and there would be other reports of mustard gas being used on 2 and 3, 7, and 9 March, which reportedly caused a total of 6,200 casualties including 1,200 dead. It was especially demoralising to the Pasdaran, who lacked any protection, and as one observed:

Martyrdom is one thing. Martyrdom with extremities blistered by mustard gas or paralysed by nerve agents is another.[23]

A more serious threat to the Iraqis emerged in the south where the Majnoon islands were assaulted, during the early hours of 23 February. At North Majnoon, Jajali led a heliborne assault by elements of 55th Brigade which established a bridgehead. Task Force 'Honain' then expanded this using Pasdaran brought in by boat despite a surprisingly determined defence by the Popular Army defenders. Task Force Badr also faced a strong defence as it staged an amphibious assault upon South Majnoon, but here, as in North Majnoon, the defenders were eventually overwhelmed by the end of 24 February to allow the Pasdaran to begin fighting their way south, and take 20 BTR APCs in the process. Meanwhile Task Force 'Hadid' successfully pushed through the marshes to enter the farmland north-east of Qurnah.[24]

Simultaneously, the Iranians frantically improved communications with the Iranian 'mainland', first using Styrofoam floats to create a 30-kilometre-long supply route to support these two task forces and Task Force 'Hadid'. The IRIA engineers with their bulldozers were joined by Pasdaran engineers, and the men of two Pasdaran divisions, to create a causeway to the main supply base at Talaiyeh. This was extended into North Majnoon by the 15-kilometre 'Khyber (pontoon) Bridge', created from pressurised Styrofoam floatation sections and light metal plates'.[25]

To shield this work, Task Force Fath struck south-west towards the Ghuzail on 23 to 24 February to hit the defensive line from the north, while the IRIA's Task Force Zeid sent its two Pasdaran divisions against the eastern defences which they managed to penetrate. Three days of fierce fighting followed and the Pasdaran tried to bring up their armour, but on 26 February the 6th Armoured Division with 65th Commando Brigade counter-attacked and drove them back. The Pasdaran renewed their attack on the night from 27 to 28 February and again fought their way through the defences in several places only to be driven back once more by 1 March. The Iraqi success made work on the land-route to North Majnoon hazardous, although it continued under enemy fire, and owed much to a combination of armour and overwhelming artillery fire while both sides' aircraft were extremely active over this sector, the Iraqis claiming 34 AFVs on 24 February alone.

The Iraqi success made work on bridging the route to North Majnoon extremely hazardous and until the route was complete it was impossible to advance upon the Nashwah Bridge. To maintain the initiative the IRIAA deployed more than 100 helicopters, mostly Bell 214/Agusta-Bell 205 augmented by six CH-47C and even a few Sikorsky S-61s and the hovercraft of the Islamic Republic of Iran Navy (IRIN), to bring some 2,000 troops onto the Majnoons on 25 February. The IrAAC hit back by using Hinds to interdict the dozens of small craft in the channels while transport helicopters inserted special forces detachments to harass the attackers. The Pasdaran reacted by deploying teams with SA-7 MANPADS, while Oerlikon twin 35mms and Soviet twin 23 mm guns were installed on firm ground on the banks of the marshes and during the day they claimed eight helicopters. Iranian Cobra gunships meanwhile ranged deep into enemy territory hunting dug-in AFVs with some success.[26]

The reinforcements brought the total of troops around the Majnoons to some 55,000 drawn from eight brigades, as the Iranians tried to exploit their success. To the west Hadid was quickly contained by 19th Division, so that 3rd Armoured Division brought up only 6th Armoured and 418th Infantry Brigades to drive the Pasdaran back into the swamp by 25 February. Attempts by 'Honain' and Badr to push south of the marshes were contained within the Ghuzail the following day by 8th Infantry Division and 4th Mountain Division exploiting the sanctuary of the northern defensive belt. On the night from 27 to 28 February the 4th Division was attacked again by three Pasdaran divisions with armour and heavy artillery support. They pushed a salient into the division's front line but on 1 March the 6th Armoured Division again pushed them back. At the same time there was a new attack upon 8th Infantry Division and its southern neighbour, 5th Mechanised Division, but this too was stopped with heavy artillery support.

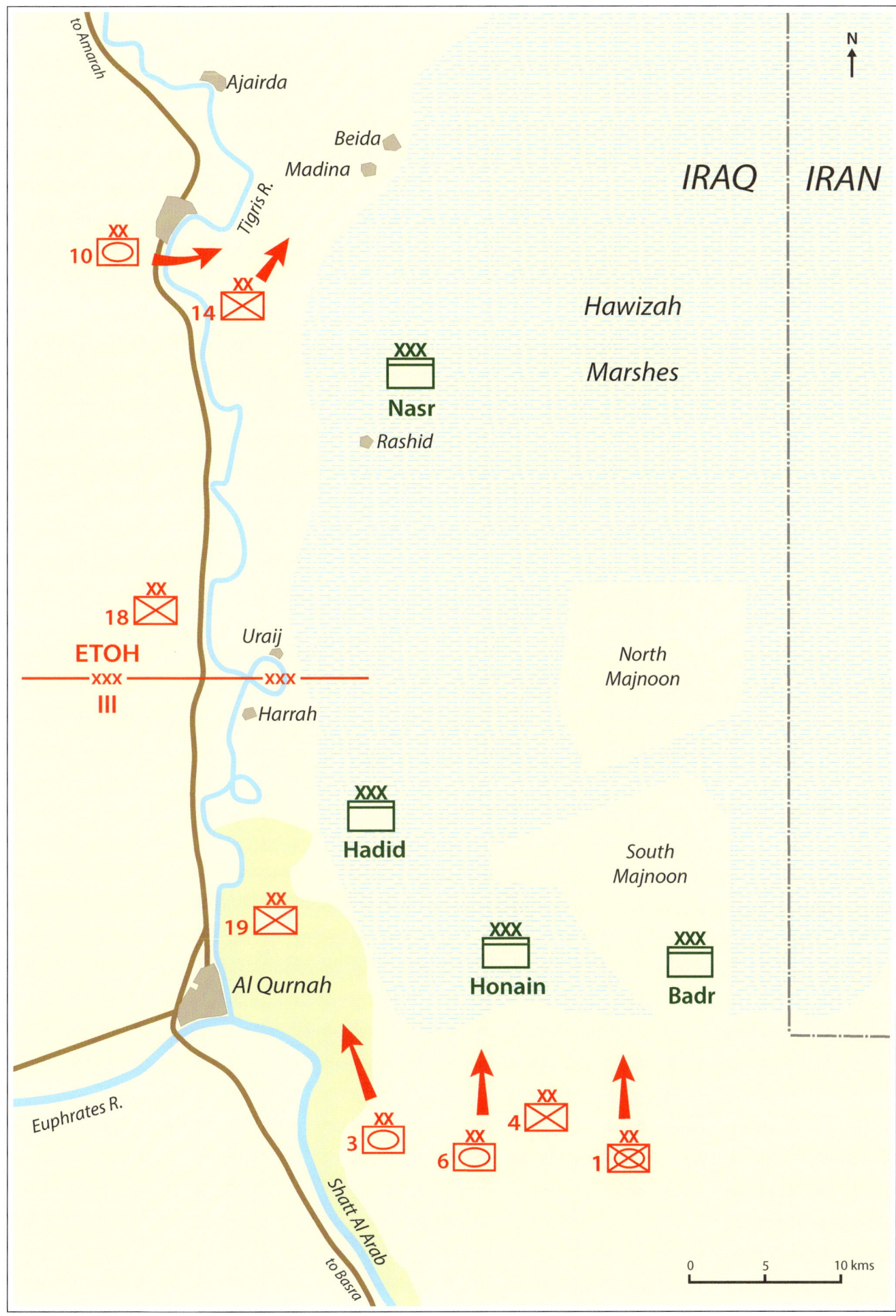

Map 3: Operation Khyber: Closing stages

Work on the 'Khyber Bridge' was completed on 29 February and the Iranians built platforms with anti-aircraft guns in the marshes, while to the east a battery of HAWK (MIM-23B) medium-range surface-to-air missiles was deployed to support IRIAF's Grumman F-14 Tomcat interceptors. Political pressure was growing on the front line commanders and Rafsanjani told the Pasdaran 'we should finish the job right here because sustaining this situation is becoming unbearable'.[27]

As Iranian supplies rolled westward they enabled a division each from 'Honain' and 'Badr' to reinforce 'Hadid' and together, on 1 March, they struck southwards after overrunning a battalion of 19th Division. Their progress towards the outskirts of Qurnah was aided by the fact that Iraqi leaders were reluctant to communicate bad news, indeed the 6th Armoured Division's commander claimed the situation was 'stable' even as his front was split; he had to abandon a number of MBTs which could not be withdrawn. This allowed the Iranians to advance far enough by the end of the day that their shells and even mortar bombs were falling on the outskirts of Qurnah, leading Baghdad to fear it might fall. To prevent this, General Makki, unable to contact Rashid, on his own initiative ordered 6th Armoured Division to send part of its reconnaissance battalion and a battalion of 25th Mechanised Brigade to secure the city. Simultaneously the remaining task forces facing III Corps renewed pressure upon the Iraqi line. As he became aware of the threat, Rashid committed 3rd Armoured Division's 6th Armoured Brigade and hastily despatched reinforcements from 6th Armoured Division and 1st Mechanised Division, together with 701st Infantry Brigade, while the IrAAC's 3rd Wing was ordered to concentrate upon this threat; with the latter flying 252 sorties that day, and the IrAF another 193, the IRIAF – which flew only 20 combat air patrols behind the lines to intercept enemy strike aircraft – was hopelessly overwhelmed. Meanwhile, the Pasdaran advance took them literally into the cannon's mouth for there were numerous battery positions and armoured vehicle laagers organised for all-round defence. But the attackers made little attempt to co-ordinate operations, indeed most of the orders were extremely vague.[28]

Too many Pasdaran batteries were supporting the infantry with direct fire operations and few tried to isolate the battlefield, due to shortages of weapons, ammunition and 'intelligence gathering systems.' The Pasdaran lacked armour and soft-skinned vehicles, which meant progress on foot across the open desert was painfully slow and exposed to enemy air attack, the Iraqis flying 212 fixed-wing and 170 rotary-wing sorties this day. The IrAF deployed Dassault Mirage F.1EQs with Saudi-provided 500kg (1,000lbs) bombs fitted with South African Jupiter fuses. According to both sides' accounts this combination proved highly effective against Iranian infantry in the open. Anticipating the problem, Najaf sent bulldozers behind the advancing infantry with orders to consolidate the day's gains by building berms. But by the end of the day they were in a salient exposed to fire from three sides as Iraqi aircraft picked off their supporting tanks and ZSU-23-4 self-propelled anti-aircraft guns.[29]

Hadid's commanders had hoped the enemy would be under pressure from the east, for as Badr moved out the northern defensive belt was struck by Task Forces Fath and Zeid, spearheaded by the Mohammad Rasoolallah and Imam Hussain Divisions respectively, while the 92nd Armoured Division tried to push through the defensive belt. The sheer scale of the assault – some 35,000 troops – surprised the defenders of the 19th Infantry and 8th Infantry Divisions, but their fortifications held this assault. The only Iranian success was a drive by their armour into the flank of the 5th Mechanised Division, which – reportedly – 'inflicted heavy losses', before running out of ammunition and withdrawing for resupply. In turn, the Imam Hussain Division took such heavy losses that it was stopped dead, leaving Task Force Fath to carry the burden, just as Iraqi air power struck its base at Talaiyeh inflicting damage and casualties.

At dawn on 2 March the Iraqis launched a set-piece armour-tipped counter-offensive, using mustard gas (and possibly Sarin nerve gas), and supported by 140 helicopter sorties, to relieve the pressure on Qurnah, which drove Pasdaran back into the marshes during the morning. However, Rashid's mechanised superiority was neutralised by the terrain which allowed the Iranians to retained control of the bunds and patches of dry ground, including the Majnoons, although he did establish a bridgehead on south-western corner of South Majnoon. In the recriminations following this disaster, the Pasdaran blamed the Army for inadequate support of the attack in the Ghuzail area as replacements, 1,500 from Tehran alone, flooded south.

Saddam closes the battle

The Iraqis now sought to regain the Majnoons but had to pause to re-organise their forces. They also flooded part of the marshes, together with some salt-flats, but the Iranians anticipated this and assembled light pontoon bridges to augment their floating bridges and bring in reinforcements. They would use the bridges, boats in the channels and even motorcycles on the bunds to conduct a mobile, aggressive, infantry-based defence, although they had to disperse their forces to avoid Iraqi artillery fire.

Rashid's offensive, spearheaded by 6th Armoured Division, began on 6 March supported by armour and helicopters, the latter flying 390 sorties on the first two days, and interdicting the channels and claiming 20 boats. The defenders consisted of a brigade of 28th IRIA Infantry Division with a Pasdaran brigade, and the marshes restricted the Iraqi advance to narrow causeways where it was vulnerable to enemy anti-armour weapons, yet the Iranians were unable to exploit this advantage.

By 12 March, the Iraqis had succeeded in establishing a bridgehead in the south-eastern corner of Southern Majnoon to secure the easiest westwards approach Baghdad-Basra highway. At this point, Saddam decided to close down the battle, less out of concern for casualties and more from the recognition he lacked sufficiently trained, and self-confident, infantry for the task. He and Rashid also recognised that the bridgehead was extremely exposed and had to be heavily fortified, but the routes into it were exposed to raids by parties of infiltrating Pasdaran. In an effort to secure their communications, a variety of sensors were deployed together with night sights and even searchlights, while electrical cables were run into the water to deter raiders. There was the usual post-offensive squabbling in which the commander of Task Force Faths' Mohammad Rasoolallah Division, Haj Mohammad Ebrahim Hemnat and his deputy Akbar Zojaji were mortally wounded, on 15 March 1984.

During the rest of the month the Iranians maintained pressure upon the sector and even brought in the 92nd Armoured Division at Ghuzail, but this had no more success than the IRGC. The Iranians consolidated their position on the Majnoon Islands and prepared to launch another offensive to take Qurnah. By April 300,000 men had been assembled – but, heavy air strikes and artillery bombardments 'destroyed the combat effectiveness and crushed the morale' of these, especially in South Majnoon.[30]

Pasdaran units left the island without permission while IRIA units had to be replaced three times. The final straw came from late March when the Iraqis diverted the flood waters from the Tigris into the western and southern edges of the marshes. Iranian engineers used sandbags, metal plates, gabions (baskets of stones and earth) and riprap (a loose assemblage of broken stones erected in water or soft ground as a foundation) and dug drainage canals leading into the Karun River. But from 5 April up to half of South Majnoon was flooded, partly due to the failure of a levee on its southwest edge of the island, forcing the Iranians to remove their armour and artillery and giving the Iraqis control of some 20% of the dry land.[31]

So ended the confusing Operation Khyber – also called 'The Second Battle East of Basra' by the Iraqis – which crippled the Iranians and prevented them from staging any significant offensives for the rest of the year. Khyber played to the strengths of the Pasdaran, their ability to traverse terrain regarded as 'impassable' to most armies and then to infiltrate and to storm defences. However, and although Iranian planning showed continued improvement, little thought was given to exploiting the initial successes and, more importantly, countering the enemy's tank-tipped response. They had tried to overcome firepower by guile and numerical superiority but failed despite sound planning by the IRIA.

The Iraqis commented:

> While the Iranians often scored impressive initial gains, they tended to bunch indecisively once they reached their first objective and they advanced into the killing zones established by Iraq's fixed defence positions and supporting artillery. Thousands of Iranians died pointlessly in this fashion between the first Iranian offensive in mid February and the end of March.[32]

Predictably the Pasdaran and their political allies in Tehran blamed the IRIA for the failure which they stated was due to the failure to storm the Fish Lake defences.

The Iraqis had recovered rapidly from their surprise, made a rapid appreciation of the situation, reacted quickly and concentrated their forces and firepower on the key areas. After the operation the Iraqis extended their defences, created artificial lakes, flooded the area on both sides of the southern section of the border and dug water tunnels under the Baghdad-Basra highway and the eastern road embankment to exploit the waters of the Tigris for emergency flooding. Yet the nerves of the Iraqi High Command were very raw and that they grew panicky, leading to the use of mustard gas and possibly the nerve agent Tabun on a wider scale; twice against the major supply bases and twice to overcome persistent defence in the Majnoons. The fact that the Iranians were moving slowly on foot made the use of mustard gas especially effective for it is a persistent poison.

The experience gained by the Iraqi Army was to be distributed rapidly and General Makki was appointed head of the Combat Development Directorate (Muderiat at-Tatweer al-Kitali) which had been established 10 years earlier and was responsible for all military publications, and now had the opportunity to provide formations and the training organisation with the latest lessons. He was succeeded at III Corps by the Shia Major General Fawzi Hamid al-Ali who would defect after the war when sent on a defence course to India. To the north the ETOH was strengthened by creating 35th Infantry Division from some task forces which became brigades.

The Americans estimated that 7,000 Iraqis and 20,000 Iranians died during Khyber. 'Lessons' estimated total Iraqi casualties at 16,000-18,000, including 6,000 dead and 1,140 prisoners, and Iranian casualties at 46,000-56,000 (including 20,000 Pasdaran killed and 20-30,000 wounded). Other sources suggested 40,000 Iranian casualties (15,000 in the first phase) to 9,000 Iraqi, while Ward suggested the IRIA suffered 6,000 dead and the Pasdaran formations 'at least twice that or even 20,000'. Once again it demonstrated a lesson which Tehran was reluctant to learn, that the Iraqis always held the upper hand against the poorly delivered Iranian attacks and eventually the Iranians lost thousands, in exchange for relatively worthless land. It also demonstrated the strategic dilemma facing both sides and the way the war was shaping. Iran had the man-power, but not the material, to support it, while Iraq had the material but lacked manpower which could be used more efficiently through the use of fortifications.

Khyber brought total Iranian casualties after four years to 510,000 including 170,000 dead, while Iraq had suffered 230,000, including 80,000 dead.[33] It provoked new discussions within the SDC and the government on the way forward, and whether or not the Pasdaran should continue major offensives relying on numerical superiority, or should it be used more efficiently in a war of attrition.[34] Rezai still believed the fervour of his men would carry them through and as late as 3 June 1986, he broadcasted:

> We do not need advanced aircraft and tanks for victory. Employment of infantry forces with light weapons, four times more than the number of Iraqi troops, will be enough for Iran to overcome the enemy.

Nevertheless, the IRGC clearly needed reforms and immediately after Khyber held a seminar, Bonyan-e Marsus ('The Packed Wall'), which reviewed the logistical and manpower arrangements during Khyber. In an acrimonious debate it was decided to rationalise the administrative organisation, reducing the 11 existing regions to five regionally-based directorates. This reform was introduced starting in September 1984. Command and control problems were also addressed, and in particular the structure of the brigades with Khyber demonstrating – as European armies discovered during the Great War – that smaller brigades were better. Correspondingly, during the year all IRGC's brigades were reduced from six to three or four battalions. This new organization was to be subjected to its first test in the next offensive in the marshes.[35]

3
THE SLOUGH OF DESPOND

For nine months the Hawizah Marshes remained a relatively dormant front with the occasional clash between patrols, raids, exchanges of artillery or mortar fire, and helicopter sweeps. However, the Iraqi situation on the Majnoon bridgehead remained precarious and after nine months Saddam attempted to improve it.

The Iraqi Army had now opted for an active defence policy which included limited offensives to improve its positions, aided by a massive arms-spending spree, much of which was funded by oil-rich Gulf States and Saudi Arabia. Fears of an enemy offensive north of the marshes around al-Amarah in the first two months of 1985 saw six such operations, including one in Rashid's III Corps area to regain South Majnoon defended by 3rd Brigade/28th Division, IRIA and Pasdaran companies.

The assault force, drawn from the 49th Infantry Brigade of the new 31st Infantry Division and 28th Brigade/8th Infantry Division – supported by the 65th Commando Brigade – was quietly assembled and a powerful artillery barrage was laid down during the early hours of 28 January 1985. With armoured support the Iraqis struck along the dry corridor between two flooded areas to pin down the defenders, while commandos in assault craft attacked from the flanks and together they recaptured several kilometres of South Majnoon and then held the administrative area in the west against counter-attacks. However, the Iranians retained a bridgehead in South Majnoon, and artillery in North Majnoon constantly harassed the new re-conquered territory.

The Iranian response was surprisingly muted, but if Baghdad believed this was due to exhaustion it would soon discover the enemy were conserving their resources. In Tehran a bitter battle of words continued over strategy between the professionals, spearheaded by the IRIA, and the clerical amateurs, including the Pasdaran, who damned the IRIA for Khyber's' failure. Both recognised that Iran's continued numerical superiority in manpower meant it retained the initiative, but the IRIA was acutely aware of Iran's weakness in the arbiters of conventional warfare; armour, artillery and air power, and favoured limited offensives. The clerics, recognising the political kudos of success, dismissed these reservations in favour of a large scale offensive, and eventually carried the day to forge a new strategy in which Iran would launch strikes which would stretch enemy resources to breaking point then seek a decisive operation.

Offensives were launched up and down the front, but the main blow was again being prepared in the Hawizah Marshes for, despite the appalling losses during Khyber,

On the first day of Operation Badr, 11 March 1985, the Iranians infiltrated the defences and established bridgeheads on the firm ground west of the Hoveyzeh Marshes. Here an exhausted platoon of Pasdaran is taking a welcome rest behind a berm. The radio operator with his distinctive aerial was an obvious target for Iraqis. (Albert Grandolini Collection)

News of the Iranian success on the first day travelled like wildfire among their troops. Here a returning boat crew passes on the glad tidings to boatloads of reinforcements sailing rapidly past the reed beds. (Albert Grandolini Collection)

Rezai and his supporters in Tehran regarded that operation as a cup half full rather than one which was half empty. With the 'Khyber Bridge' still intact and their communications within the marshes steadily improved this boded well for a renewed offensive in the region which would be launched later. The plan was now to strike towards the end of the rainy season in March, when an average of 32mm of rain falls, but before April, when the average tends to fall away.

Both sides prepare

During the first months of the year, and shielded by the rains from enemy air power and artillery, a stream of boats built up men and supplies in the myriad of muddy islets where reed banks shielded them from terrestrial observation both visual and by battlefield surveillance radar, as well as from aircraft (although listening posts could detect their engines). The task was eased by the reluctance of the Iraqi Popular Army, supported by Border Guards and the Navy, to patrol aggressively, indeed they were usually content to remain in their bases during the rain or make nominal patrols. By contrast up to six months beforehand the Iranians aggressively patrolled by boat to push the Iraqis out of the marshes onto dry land. From September the Iranians began extensive engineering work in anticipation of an offensive, building roads and bases east of the marshes and within them flood control measures, as well as further strengthening their logistics by reinforcing the 'Khyber Bridge' route with a second 'stout causeway' to North Majnoon. The network was later expanded through the marshes both by IRIA engineers and the Pasdaran 46th 'Al-Hadi' Engineer Brigade, with pontoon bridges, causeways and narrow footbridges for resupply, and to support the planned offensive. This supported a strong Iranian military presence within the marshes even after Badr.[1]

Outline planning for the offensive began late in 1984 to produce a more ambitious version of Khyber, whose goals were to cut the Baghdad-Basra highway between Amarah and Qurnah, exploiting six bridges over the Tigris including three 60-tonne military bridges, and a fourth over the Euphrates on the outskirts of Qurnah. This

Boat-loads of IRGC-troops preparing to embark in the fleet of 'little boats' whose sole protection was this 14.5mm KVP machine gun, manned by an elderly, white-bearded Pasdaran. (Tom Cooper Collection)

The Iranian 'small boat flotilla' did not just deliver men and supplies but always returned with wounded or carrying Iraqi prisoners – like this group of unfortunates. Some 1,500 Iraqi soldiers were captured during Badr. (Albert Grandolini Collection)

would leave the Iranians ready to envelop Basra from the north and from the east, then storm the city. It was also aimed to secure the Majnoons for fear the enemy would use them as a springboard for a renewed attack across the border. These fears were fed by the Iraqi attack on 28 January which established a bridgehead within them. This operation appears to have acted as a catalyst to accelerate Iranian detailed planning, which was apparently completed by 20 February to become Operation Badr.[2]

The execution of the operation was assigned by the Khatam al-Anbiya Headquarters, which divided its total of 115,000 troops into two joint task forces; the IRGC's Najaf, commanded by Colonel Manouchehr Dejkam, and IRIA's Karbala, under Colonel Hossein Hassani-Sa'di. In the first phase the two task forces were to advance through the marshes to secure jump-off positions on the firm ground to the west, around Uzayr, and south. Najaf

Worn out by intensive operations of the first two years of war, and lacking replacement aircraft, the IRIAF was incapable of providing more close air support for such offensives as Badr than a total of about 40 air strikes. This photograph shows a two-seat F-5F leading a single-seat F-5E into an attack, at an altitude that was typical for Iranian pilots in this war. (Tom Cooper Collection)

As usual, the IRIAA provided plentiful helicopter support to ground forces during Operation Badr. The IRIAF further reinforced this effort with the help of its own Bell 214As. (Tom Cooper Collection)

As so often before and after Operation Badr, CH-47C Chinooks of the IRIAA provided heavy-lift support for forward deployed units, and also participated in CASEVAC and MEDEVAC operations. (via Tom Cooper)

would then cross the Tigris to establish a bridgehead which would split the enemy by cutting the Baghdad-Basra highway, while Karbala would secure the Tigris cultivated area northwest of Qurnah, then a Pasdaran division would cross the Tigris and establish a bridgehead 5 kilometres deep. In both taskforces the spearhead would consist of Pasdaran, but the need to sew spring crops meant the Basiji element was severely reduced.[3]

The Pasdaran had learned many of Khyber's lessons and for once their divisions and brigades would be only partly committed. Dejkam's Task Force Najaf had some eight brigades of 5th Nasr, 7th Vali Asr, 14th Imam Hussein, 21st Imam Reza, 25th Karbala Divisions (total of 27 infantry battalions), 15th Imam Hassan and 18th al-Ghadir Infantry Brigades (5 infantry battalions), together with the whole of 77th Infantry Division, IRIA (nine battalions). According to the Iranians artillery support consisted of two gun and one MRLS battalions of the 22nd IRIA Artillery Group, one of the Pasdaran 40th Ressalat Artillery Brigade and two of Karbala Division. Nominally, this would have meant a total of 90 guns, but such accounts appear to ignore 77th Division's four battalions with another 70 tubes. Overall, Task Force Najaf included about 25,500 Pasdaran and 14,000 IRIA troops.

Hassani-Sa'di's Task Force Karbala had one of the largest concentrations of IRIA troops in the war including all of the 21st and 28th Infantry Divisions (18 infantry battalions), two brigades of 92nd Armoured Division, a brigade of 81st Armoured Division, the 55th Airborne Brigade (five battalions) and the 33rd Artillery Group with five gun-battalions and one MRLS battalion. These were reinforced by 10 brigades of 8th Najaf Ashraf, 17th Ali Ibn Abu Talib, 27th Mohammad Rasoolallah and 31st Ashura Divisions IRGC, the 44th Qamar Bani Hashem Infantry Brigade (four infantry battalions) and 72nd Moharram Armoured Brigade. Total strength was 51,000 IRIA and 26,000 Pasdaran supported by some 320 guns and about 100 MBTs. In addition the operation received support from the IRIA's 1st Brigade/23rd Special Forces Division, 49 IRIAA helicopters (two AB 206 observation, 12 Cobra gunships, 27 Bell 214/AB 205 transport, eight CH-47 medium transport), and supplies through the 1st Area Support Command. Rezai's confidence was raised by the Pasdarans' preparations for the new offensive which

While advancing southwards to the frontline along one of the Styrofoam floating pathways during Badr, these Pasdaran took time for prayers. (Tom Cooper Collection)

missiles, were augmented with many recoilless rifles; the US-made M40 and Chinese Type-75. Tehran had also addressed the chemical warfare problem and provided the Pasdaran with respirators (gas masks), chemical warfare suits as well as atropine injectors with nerve agent antidotes, and the more immediate threat of drowning was countered by providing each man with a life jacket. However, such was the rivalry with the IRIA that the Pasdaran refused to transfer surplus life jackets to the IRIA – which also complained about a shortage of trucks, although this was another perennial problem for the Iranians.[4]

While a communications infrastructure had been woven through the eastern end of the marshes, and ensured some armour and artillery could be moved forward as well as helping the establishment of a fire base on North Majnoon, the planners recognised that projecting this westwards would be difficult. The IRIN could provide hovercraft, helicopters and 150 Gemini rigid inflatable boats, but Hassani-Sa'di recognised that moving his forces, and especially armour, across the marshes and then the Tigris required more, and he estimated that he needed 34 bridges including two more 10-kilometre pre-fabricated structures. The Iraqi bridges across the Tigris were well defended, so crossing the river would require boats, bridges and hovercraft and his inventory included 490 boats, including 20 24-metre vessels, 22 BTR-50s and 150 bulldozers. Another major problem was the paucity of artillery ammunition, with sufficient for only 15 days and no more than 20 rounds per 105mm howitzer, 10-12 rounds for other 130mm, 155mm and 203mm weapons and 80 rockets per MRLS.[5]

The Iranians were also well aware that once the offensive began it would act like a starting gun with both sides racing to build up their forces. Najaf was estimated to be facing three brigades with 10 infantry, one tank and two artillery battalions, while Karbala faced 28 infantry/mechanised (six on Majnoon), three tank and seven artillery battalions (five on Majnoon). However, it was anticipated the enemy could rapidly relocate 21 brigades to face Karbala; 14 (with 55 infantry/mechanised and 14 tank battalions) within 10 hours, four (12 infantry battalions) to Qurnah and a total of 10 artillery battalions, while Najaf could face 14 manoeuvre (infantry and armour) and two artillery battalions. Afterward IRIA historians claimed they had never been optimistic about the prospects of winning this race.

would see them better equipped not only in infantry weapons but also in heavy weapons. To meet the obvious threat from enemy armour the attackers had not only numerous RPGs with a plentiful supply of rockets which, in the absence of anti-armour guided

One of the entirely new appearances on the battlefield of Operation Badr were a few T-72s operated by the IRGC. The tanks in question were all former mounts of the Iraqi 10th Armoured Brigade. They proved urgently necessary, because counterattacks by Iraqi armour crushed the desperately secured Iranian bridgehead across the Tigris. (Tom Cooper Collection)

The Iraqis had learned lessons from Khyber and had substantially strengthened their defences along the Tigris. They built high observation towers to look over the banks of reeds, which were cut back and burned nearer the firm ground west of the marshes. Here a line of bunkers was constructed, each surrounded by large barbed-wire entanglements and minefields which, on the marsh edge, extended into the water. Yet the terrain dictated that these defences were extremely shallow, with

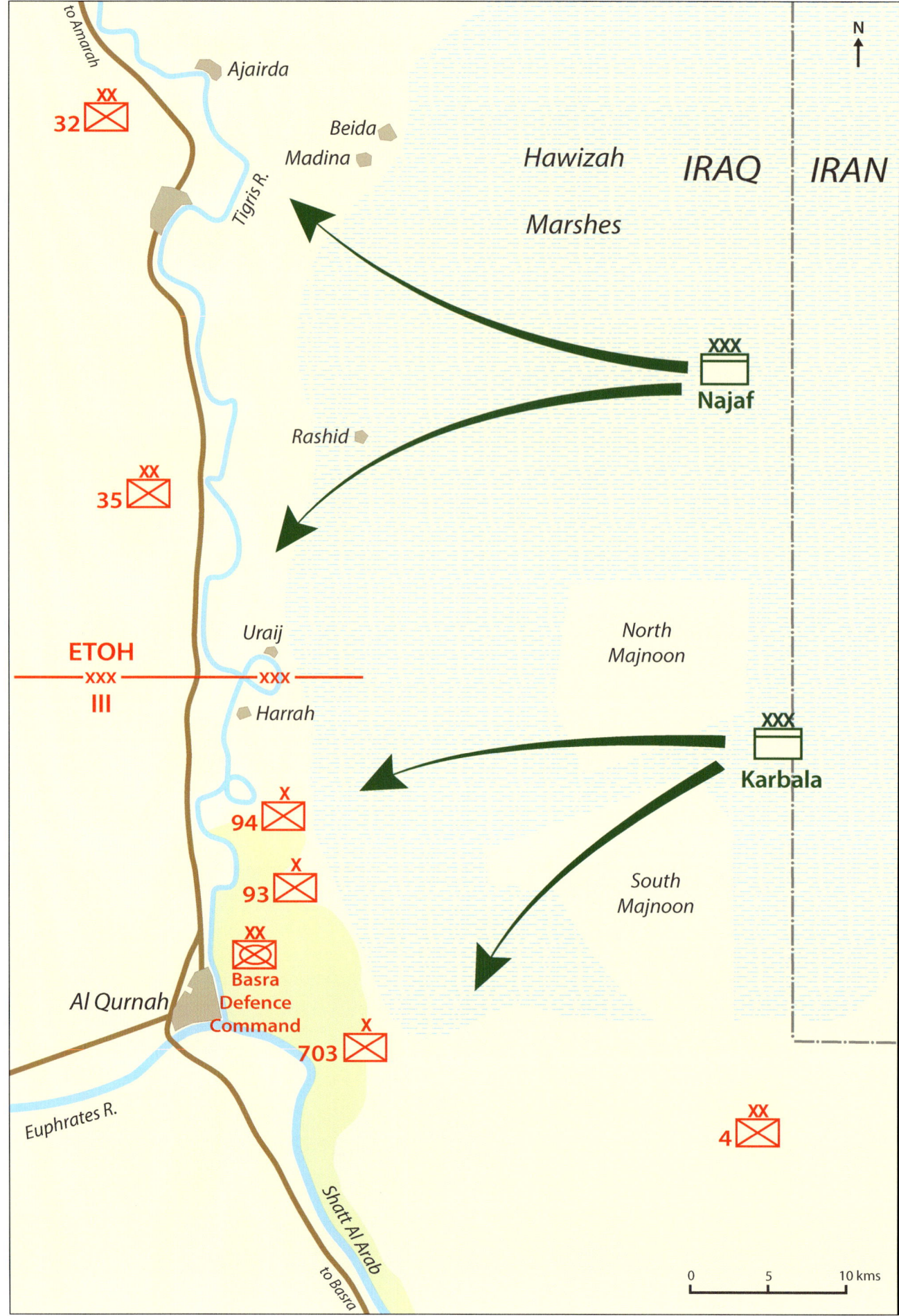

Map 4: Operation Badr: Opening stages

command posts and artillery all vulnerable to infiltration. A fortnight before the Iranian attack warnings, the defenders were alerted that it might be imminent and there was frantic work building a similar second line along the river's western bank, focusing upon potential crossing points on the river covered by artillery batteries. Anti-landing obstacles were installed at vulnerable sites such as Beida, which had been demolished the previous year, and the Iraqis could also flood large areas in and around the marshes. The blow would land upon the ETOH, now under Brigadier Mohammad Abdul Qadir, after Fakhri returned to Baghdad as Deputy Chief of Staff for Operations. Qadir was regarded as a brave and very efficient staff officer but had no close relationship with Saddam and whose relationship with the foul-mouthed III Corps commander, Rashid, was strained.[6] Its TAOR stretched from south of al-Amarah, along the marsh's western banks to the borders of Maysan and Basra Provinces on the 31st Parallel, with 32nd and 35th Infantry Divisions, which were formed after Khyber had been contained, and Basra Defence Command under Brigadier Ihsan Kamel Shibib, which covered Qurnah, while 66th Commando Brigade was nearby but not under his command. Each consisted of a single infantry brigade and

A closed down T-55 operated by the IRGC moving forward, ready for one of the usually deadly Iraqi counterattacks during Badr. (Tom Cooper Collection)

A ZSU-23-4 Shilka of the IRIA seen in position and expecting an incoming Iraqi air strike. The weapon proved a formidable foe to low-flying fixed-wing and rotary-wing aircraft during the Iran-Iraq War, but also highly effective when deployed against exposed infantry formations. (Tom Cooper Collection)

the equivalent of another in Popular Army units, Brigadier Major General Karim ad-Dabbagh's 35th Infantry Division (formed from Border Guards) which faced Task Force Najaf had only 429th Infantry Brigade augmented by naval coast defence forces equivalent to a brigade, five battalion-size Popular Army sectors and the battalion-strong Marshes Command Forces (Quiadet Quwat Al-Ahwar), a total of some 9,000 men and some 40 guns, and a tank battalion with some 40 MBTs. Shibib, who covered the marshes in Basra Province, had north-to-south, the 94th, 93rd, and 703rd Infantry Brigades with only 18 artillery batteries and one MRLS battery, a total of some 12,000 men and 114 guns and MRLS, while his reaction force was the 66th Commando Brigade. His command did not include an artillery commander and when the Iranian attack began, Qadir assigned him an artillery liaison officer to help co-ordinate fire plans. Qadir's plan, worked out with the aid of Army Chief-of-Staff General Abd al-Jawad Thanun, was to give ground in the centre but hold the flanks, to contain the enemy on the fringes of the marshes and erode his strength with artillery and air power which would then support a counter-attack. The plan was approved by Defence Minister Khairallah and, more importantly, by Saddam himself. Notably, no counter-attack forces were assigned to Qadir, but in the north Major General Sabih Umran al-Tarfih's 10th Armoured Division (17th Armoured, 24th and 27th Mechanised Brigades), and the 68th Commando Brigade with some 15,000 troops and 170 MBTs were available. Furthermore, Rashid's III Corps had the usual complement, including the 3rd and 6th Armoured and 5th Mechanised Divisions in reserve – the last having finally been withdrawn from static defensive duties and replaced by the newly-established 30th Infantry Division. Brigadier Abd al-Karim Mahmud al-Ithaw's 4th Mountain Infantry Division was on Rashid's left where its 5th Mountain Brigade and 18th Infantry Brigade would be committed to the battle.[7]

The Chieftain Mk. 5/3P remained the major MBT in Iranian service during the mid-1980s. However, with the IRGC taking over the brunt of fighting on the frontlines, IRIA formations equipped with the type were held back in reserve, and thus their Chieftains saw ever less action. While still wearing the standard camouflage colour of light olive green, applied since the 1970s, this was badly worn out on most of vehicles. Indeed, by 1986 most of the surviving Chieftains barely showed even their national insignia - applied in the form of a roundel in Iranian national colours on turret sides and the rear storage box. (Artwork by Radek Panchartek)

Iranian M60A1s damaged early during the war were gradually repaired and often re-painted, usually in yellow-sand overall, although the exact shade of the colour in question remains hard to gauge: most of the available photographs show them covered by a thick layer of mud and dust. National markings were still regularly applied on the turret sides, but most seem not to have worn any other insignia. (Artwork by Radek Panchartek)

This ex-Iraqi T-62 was captured during one of the offensives in 1982, overhauled, re-painted in two shades of green, and brought to service by one of the IRGC's armoured brigades. Notable is the identification marking on the gun tube, and the – almost usual – religiously motivated quotation from the Qoran. (Artwork by Radek Panchartek)

As long as they survived long enough, captured Iraqi T-54/-55s were all overhauled or repaired and re-painted before being pressed into service by the IRGC. Their usual new colour consisted of yellow-sand only, but most wore not only a large IRGC logo in red, but also various inscriptions. In this case, this is a verse from the Quran. (Artwork by Radek Panchartek)

This formerly Iraqi BMP-1 was captured while still wearing a relatively fresh coat of olive green overall, probably the colour in which it was delivered from the USSR. It received the IRGC logo, and the inscription 'Islamic Revolutionary Guards Corps' hastily sprayed in white along the side of the hull. (Artwork by Radek Panchartek)

Iran acquired ZSU-57-2s from the USSR in the late 1960s, and then captured additional examples from Iraq during the war. This vehicle retained the original khaki-green colour applied on all vehicles of the Iranian army before the war, as well as the national marking applied on turret sides. The ZSU-57-2 included two 57mm S-60 anti-aircraft guns installed in an open-top turret, mounted on the T-54 chassis. The guns could elevate up to 85 degrees and were fed from four-round clips. Lack of radar control made them fair-weather weapons, but they proved deadly opponents for helicopters. (Artwork by Radek Panchartek)

Iran acquired 100 ZSU-23-4s directly from the Soviet Union in 1969. They served with air defence regiments attached to each of the Army's divisions. All were painted in light olive green overall, and had national insignia applied on hull sides. Like other vehicles of the regular Iranian Army, they should have received four-digit serial numbers - applied in black on the hull front and the rear - but, sadly, no details about these are known. (Artwork by Radek Panchartek)

A number of M113A1s and M113A2s originally acquired by Iran from the USA in the 1970s were converted through the addition of the 'mast' for BGM-71 TOW ATGMs during the war with Iraq, and officially re-designated as M150. As the inscription on its hull side indicates, this vehicle was subsequently assigned to the 201 A'emeh Anti-Armour Unit. This was a dedicated anti-armour unit of the IRGC, using Army equipment handed over to the Pasdaran. Established in 1983, it was expanded to a full brigade by 1987. Note that the artwork shows the BGM-71 TOW launcher unloaded. (Artwork by Radek Panchartek)

Following the successful performance of 10th Armoured Brigade's T-72s early during the war, Iraq placed orders for 250 T-72M1s in Poland, followed by up to 1,000 additional T-72Ms and T-72M1s imported from Czechoslovakia and the USSR. Many went into the battles of the mid-1980s still wearing olive green overall, as on delivery. Some yellow sand (often bleached into light grey by sun and sand) was crudely applied on some examples, as illustrated here - and before the entire fleet was re-painted in that colour, later on. (Artwork by Radek Panchartek)

A reconstruction of an Iraqi T-55 from Polish production. The vehicle was equipped with typical, Polish-made storage box on the turret side, but also a dozer blade and an infra-red reflector. The camouflage pattern consisted of yellow-sand and blue-green, as usual. The Iraqis purchased several hundreds of such tanks during the war with Iran, initially because of Soviet refusals to re-supply Baghdad, and latter because the Soviets were unable to deliver the number of tanks demanded by Iraq. Reportedly, the Iraqis found Polish-built tanks slightly better than those made in the USSR, but not as good as those made in former Czechoslovakia. (Artwork by Radek Panchartek)

A reconstruction of one of about 400 Chinese-made Type-69 MBTs (improved T-54, including a 100mm dual-axis stabilized, smoothbore gun; a laser rangefinder, and a new 580hp engine). The vehicles in question were acquired in the period 1983-1985 in order to replace losses from the first two years of war with Iran. As in the case of all the T-54s and T-55s operated by the Iraqi Army of the 1980s, they were camouflaged in standard colours of yellow-sand and blue-green, but most wore side-skirts made of rubber too. No turret-numbers or any other kind of insignia is known to have been applied: although many Type-69s were seen and photographed by international journalists underway in the Faw area of 1986, most had their turrets full of the crew's personal belongings and ammunition boxes. (Artwork by Radek Panchartek)

Clear photographs of Iraqi ZSU-57-2s remain relatively rare and thus very little is known about their camouflage patterns and insignia. This artwork is based on several stills from a TV-documentary published in Iraq in the early 1980s, and showing an example apparently painted in yellow sand, with stripes of blue-green applied in zig-zag pattern down all four sides of the turret. (Artwork by Radek Panchartek)

Only three out of the first 140 AH-1Js built for Iran were modified to the full configuration compatible with BGM-71 TOW ATGMs before the fall of the Shah in 1979, and thus the majority of the fleet serves until today armed with the 20mm M197 gun, and 3.75 inch unguided rockets only. All are painted in dark yellow-sand and dark earth over, and pale grey under. The original crest of the IIAA (applied below the cockpit) was usually replaced by the so-called 'Onion' – the official crest of the Islamic Republic of Iran in the form of a stylized word 'Allah', applied in red or white in the same place. Service titles were often applied not only in two different positions but also in two different colours, as shown here. (Artwork by Tom Cooper)

When the Iranian Army depleted its stocks of BGM-71 TOW anti-tank missiles, the idea was born to install AGM-65A Maverick, electro-optically guided air-to-surface missiles on some of IRIAA's AH-1Js instead. This modification proved successful and was deployed in combat. The AGM-65As taken over by the Army for this purpose were usually crudely over-sprayed with green colour in order to make them less conspicuous. The AH-1J depicted here is otherwise wearing the standard camouflage pattern of dark yellow-sand and dark earth, and usual national and service insignia, though with its 'Onion' applied in white. Notable is the replacement frame for the front cockpit hood, left in forest green. (Artwork by Tom Cooper)

A reconstruction of a Bell 214A Esfahan of an unknown IRIAA unit, as seen in the Abadan area in 1986. By the time of the Iran-Iraq War, this helicopter received the full service title applied in the usual place on the cabin doors, and the 'Onion' in black. Early during the war, many of the IRIAA's Bell 214As went into combat still wearing the 'last three' of their serials applied in large orange digits on the top of the nose and cabin doors. Notable is that the top sides of the main rotor blades on all helicopters of this type were painted dark yellow-sand too. (Artwork by Tom Cooper)

Between 1977 and 1984, the IrAF, and then the IrAAC received a total of 35 SA.342L, 56 SA.342K and 20 SA.342H Gazelle helicopters. Most received the camouflage pattern depicted here, consisting of sand, chocolate brown and olive drab on upper surfaces and sides, and light blue under. More than 80 saw combat service during the war with Iran, but their attrition was heavy because their 'glasshouse' type of cockpit proved vulnerable even to small-arms fire from the ground. Usual armament consisted of four HOT ATGMs, but 20mm cannons (installed on the right side only), and various pods for unguided rockets (usually 68mm) saw widespread service too. (Artwork by Tom Cooper)

The Mi-25 was probably the best-known helicopter gunship in IrAAC service during the war with Iran. At least two batches of 12 helicopters each were delivered to Iraq: one in 1980 (known serials in range 2110-2119) and another in 1984 or 1985 (serials in range 4493 and upwards). All were camouflaged in standard pattern for Mi-25s exported to a number of foreign customers, including Afghanistan, Libya, Nicaragua, and Mozambique, and consisting of yellow sand and green on upper surfaces and sides, and light admiralty grey (BS381C/697) on bottom surfaces. Their 9M17P Falanga (AT-2 Swatter) anti-tank missiles were usually painted in dark olive green. Other frequently deployed armament consisted of UB-32-57 pods for 57mm unguided rockets. (Artwork by Tom Cooper)

A reconstruction of an Iraqi Mi-8T as seen on a photograph from the early 1980s, too poor for reproduction. This helicopter - said to have been frequently used for deployment of Iraqi special forces behind Iranian frontlines - was apparently delivered wearing the usual olive green colour on upper surfaces and sides, and light admiralty grey (BS381C/697) on bottom sides, and then camouflaged through application of irregular splotches of sand and apple green. Unusually, no large Iraqi national flag was applied on the rear of the cabin: instead, it received only a single set of national markings, and a small serial (2062) in black on the boom. As often in the case of Iraqi Mi-8s, rear cargo doors were completely removed, in order to enable rapid embarkation and disembarkation of troops and cargo. (Artwork by Tom Cooper)

The crew of this IRGC-operated BMP-1 optimistically cheered to the cameraman, while their vehicle was moving forward in a cloud of dust to counter another of the Iraqi counterattacks. (Tom Cooper Collection)

The crew of an Iraqi 105mm Oto-Melara Model 56 pack howitzer rest in their position while the gun captain is on the telephone, conferencing with superiors. The Model 56 was used by light batteries to augment the normal divisional artillery, which primarily consisted of 122mm howitzers and 130mm guns. (Albert Grandolini Collection)

Corps together with EOTH. Four days later a new Pasdaran division was identified east of the marshes but the arrival of two brigades for 77th Division led the GMID, on 10 March, to confirm its conclusion that the Fish Lake was the primary objective. Later in the day the Nasr, Vali Asr' and Karbala Divisions were observed near the marshes and several brigades were observed to join them.[8]

These were the spearheads of Task Force Najaf but, in a face-saving report on 25 March, the GMID would bewail the fact that Iraqi COMINT failed to provide its usual cornucopia of information in terms of instructions including code words. The report unwittingly underlines the failures of Iraqi intelligence which failed to detect the presence of the enemy task force headquarters, the assembly of boats and new bridging materials, or even a build-up of artillery on North Majnoon aided by the gradual withdrawal of 2nd Brigade from the 28th Division.[9]

The malign influence of these GMID assessments meant that Baghdad's operational direction initially responded to the threat from the marshes as a diversion, indeed the IrAF priority initially remained attacks upon Iranian cities.

Operation Badr begins

On 11 March, amid a flurry or air raids and scattered artillery bombardments, Pasdaran headquarters issued the 'go code' which was 'Ya Fatimah al-Zahn' and the attack began that night at 2230 hrs. Security was paramount and when the battalions of Task Force Najaf moved into the marshes from the afternoon of 11 March, according to the Iraqi GMID, the rank-and-file were informed they were to strengthen the area's defences. Their pre-attack briefing occurred only as they received combat rations and the Pasdaran – according to the IRIA – did not inform their 'regular' colleagues that the offensive had begun until 12 March! There were three thrusts along a 10-kilometre-front between Uzayr and Qurnah using hundreds of small assault boats, fire support being provided by recoilless guns and mortars mounted on flat-bottomed boats or rafts. Heliborne forces from 55th Airborne Brigade and 23rd Special Forces Brigade were inserted on both banks of the river to harass the enemy and were reported to have captured some Soviet Scud missiles during this phase. This seems unlikely as these launchers were held far from the battlefield, but if the story is true it may refer to FROG missiles.[10]

Although there had been signs and portents of an Iranian offensive, GMID failed to provide the defending leaders with adequate warning, demonstrating the old adage that it is easy to acquire data but more difficult to analyse it. IrAF photo-reconnaissance monitored Iranian engineering work and by 9 February photographic interpreters reported this included three helicopter bases with 25 landing spots. By 21 February the GMID alerted Saddam to the fact that an offensive in the marshes was imminent and work began on strengthening the defences along the Tigris. But the Iranians succeeded in confusing GMID about the primary axes and the appearance of 77th Infantry Division headquarters and 55th Airborne Brigade together with three Pasdaran divisions (3rd 'Saheb al-Zaman', 14th 'Imam Hossein' and 19th 'Fajr') east of Basra led it to conclude on 23 February that the enemy aimed to strike the Fish Lake line. The airborne brigade's location, soon followed by detection nearby of the IRIA Special Forces brigade, seemed to confirm this idea, yet GMID remained uncertain and to cover itself it issued a preliminary warning on 5 March to III and IV

The initial Pasdaran success, as an Iraqi after-action report of

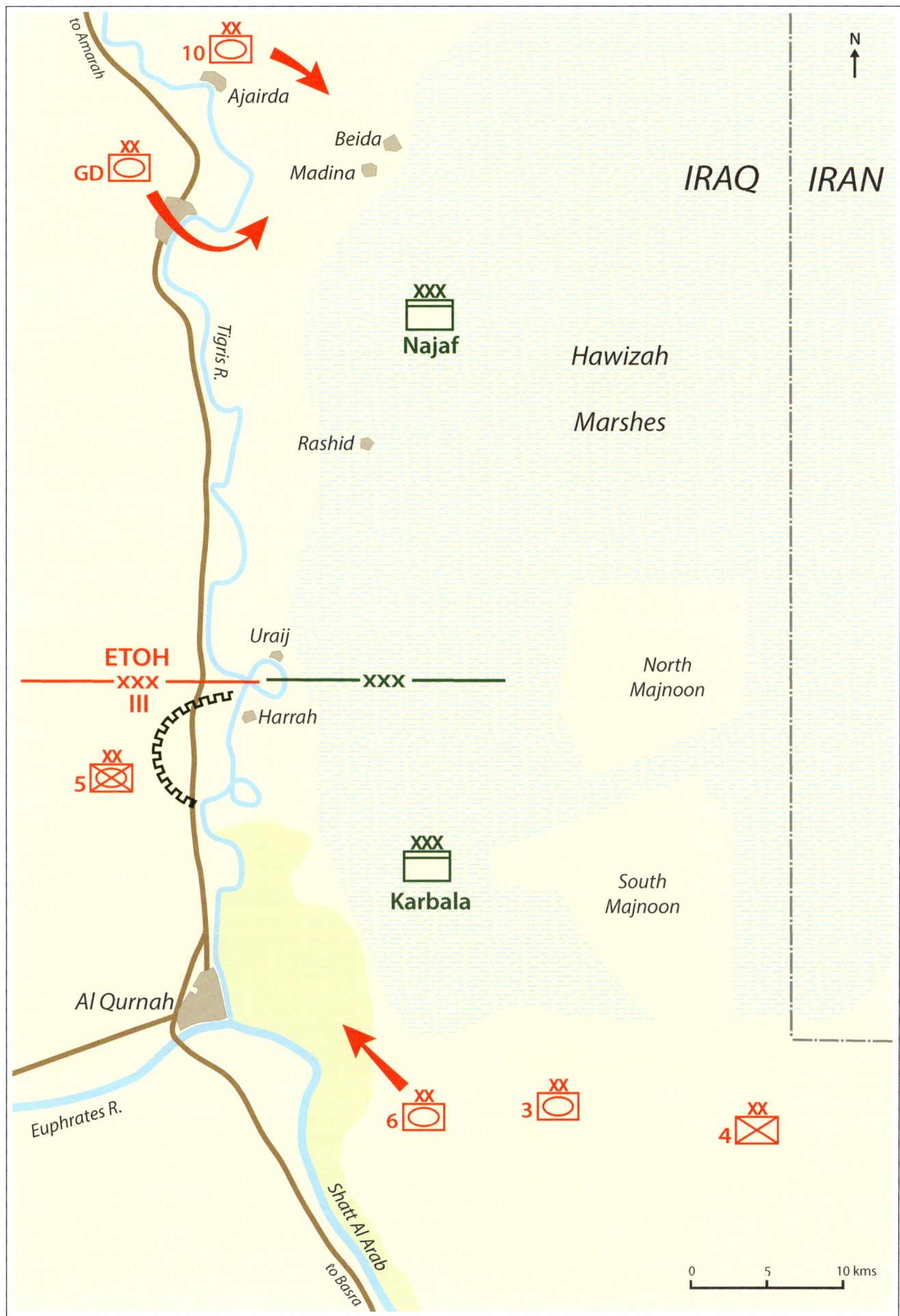

Map 5: Operation Badr: Closing stages

21-22 April noted, was due to the narrowness of the defensive belt which exposed the defenders and deprived them of a significant and well-placed reserve. This allowed the Iranians to infiltrate the numerous gaps to isolate then assault the positions, the Popular Army companies being especially vulnerable, although it appears that Shibib's 94th Brigade was virtually destroyed in this operation. During these attacks many commanders were killed and US COMINT reported there was 'a general state of panic and chaos' which helped to clear the Pasdarans' path. Surprisingly, despite (or possibly because of) the GMID alert on 5 March, the report observed that a number of commanders, possibly only Popular Army commanders, went on leave. When he read this report Saddam might have recalled his comment in February:

> Our strength is in the awareness of our soldiers and their strength is the lack of awareness by their soldiers.[11]

Task Force Najaf' broke through to Ajairda and Rashid to control the exits from the marshes as supplies and reinforcements flowed in on a fleet of boats, while the Styrofoam pontoon bridges were used extensively for reinforcements and augmented by footbridges created by lashing rubber boats together and placing planking upon them. The Imam Hussein Division and 77th Division were deployed south of Uzayr but most of Dekjam's troops were to the north, and it was against them that Qadir promptly reacted with 429th Brigade, aided by part of 68th Commando Brigade, and counter-attacked to retake Ajairda. During 12 March the fighting in the north intensified into the evening with the arrival of Iranian reinforcements but the initiative had been lost and progress was slow. Ajairda was retaken but the Iraqi troops were conducting a fighting retreat which bought time for 10th Armoured Division to drive down the eastern bank and appear about dawn on 13 March. It counter-attacked with heavy artillery support and helped 35th Infantry Division and 66th Brigade to regain Ajairda and Uraij (Ujayrid or Uralje) south of Uzayr, while the following day it recaptured the ruins of Beida.

Task Force Karbala had the greatest success reaching the Tigris on the first day, led by IRIA's 21st Infantry Division and the IRGC's Mohammad Rasoolallah Division, but on the first evening the Pasdaran commander asked his IRIA comrade to relieve two of its seven battalions that were suffering from diarrhoea and malnutrition. On their left the hopes of the Ashura Division and 'Qamar Bani Hashem' Brigade of taking the bridges across the Tigris were thwarted by Iraqi demolitions. Behind them three lightweight pontoon bridges, one capable of carrying AFVs, were being brought through the marshes to support an assault across the Tigris. Until they arrived Hassani-Sa'di had to content himself the following day by consolidating his gains, aided by the arrival of the Ali Ibn Abu Talib Division to give him control down to the cultivated area north-east of Qurnah. But here, as elsewhere, despite significant improvements in Pasdaran logistics the Iranians still found it difficult to sustain their offensive because of the problems of bringing up heavy weapons. As the advance continued it 'also experienced growing support and logistic problems with each kilometre it advanced, and its forces became steadily better targets as they emerged out of the wetlands and onto dry land'.[12]

The bridges began to arrive on the night of 13–14 March and, as they did so, elements of the 55th Airborne Brigade and Mehdi Bakeri's Ashura Division were helicoptered across the Tigris to cut the Baghdad-Basra highway with a bridgehead up to 4 kilometres deep and 15 kilometres wide into which three battalions of the former and a brigade of the latter were inserted. This success delighted the clerics and politicians in Tehran, although the total haul of prisoners was reported by 17 March at only 1,100. It forced the Iraqis to evacuate neighbouring villages and towns as well as closing the area to civilian traffic while the Ba'ath Party in Maysan and Basra Provinces organised local defence forces based upon the Popular Army to hold towns and cities. Part of the Najaf Ashraf Division later moved into the bridgehead, which was under increasing air and artillery attack, but hopes of moving in the remainder of 55th Airborne and the Special Forces Brigades by helicopter were dashed because of enemy air superiority. The bridges and IRNL ferry service, which included a pair of hovercraft, were under heavy fire making the prospects of a Tigris crossing hazardous.[13]

Iraqi reinforcements arrive

Shibib's Basra Defence Force was ordered to prevent the enemy expanding the bridgehead while Rashid was sucked into the battle with Ithawi's 4th Mountain Division transferred northward, Brigadier Iyad al-Futayyih al-Rawi's 6th Armoured Division began to push into the cultivated area northeast of Qurnah, while Brigadier Ali Jasim al-Hayyan's 5th Mechanised Division crossed the Nashwah Bridge and prepared to advance up the west bank of the Tigris to contain the immediate threat.

On 13 March, Defence Minister Khairrallah ordered the General Staff to establish a forward headquarters at Basra under Chief-of-Staff Thanun to co-ordinate the Iraqi response. Thanun brought with him Fakhri and the Deputy Chief-of-Staff for Training, Major General Sa'adi (the former III Corps commander), together with the head of Intelligence, Brigadier Shukur Shahin (the former 6th Armoured Division commander). The headquarters was established the following day and was promptly visited by Saddam who authorised the use of the recently established Guards Division under Major General Talia Khalil ad-Duri (4th Guards Armoured and 3rd Guards Special Forces Brigades) while 4th Mountain Division was brought up from III Corps, together with 6th Armoured Division and support troops – with the 3rd Armoured Division's headquarters remaining behind the Fish Lake line. As other reinforcements were arriving Thanun drafted a plan to respond to the threat. Given Fakhri's intimate knowledge of the area and his experience at thwarting Khyber, he returned to Uzayr to assume command of the northern task force which was to crush Task Force Najaf and included the Guards Division (2nd Guards, 10th and 42nd Armoured Brigades, 4th Guards and 702nd Infantry Brigades, and Guards Emergency Force); 10th Armoured Division with its own 17th Armoured, 24th and 27th Mechanised Brigades reinforced by 5th Mountain and 29th Infantry Brigades of the 4th Mountain Division, the divisional headquarters; the 3rd Guards, 66th and 68th Commando Brigades; and the 35th Division's battered 429th Brigade. Altogether some 50,000 men with 450 MBTs.

Sa'adi established his task force headquarters in Qurnah to command the thrust from the west with 5th Mechanised (30th Armoured, 20th Mechanised, 19th Mountain Brigades, the last from the 7th Mountain Division) and the south with 6th Armoured Division (16th Armoured, 25th Mechanised and 18th Infantry Brigades), Shibib's Basra Defence Force (93th Infantry, 65th Commando and 1st Shock Troop Brigades), the headquarters and support forces of 6th Armoured Division – or some 39,000 troops with 270 MBTs. The divisional artillery was boosted by 30 medium and heavy batteries to give some 720 guns, augmented by MRLS and a Scud-B brigade (which was then not used). Unsurprisingly, the 35,000 tired Iranians, their 200 guns and a handful of MRLS were clearly outnumbered.

hit targets around the marshes. Heavy rain on 14 March reduced operations, but then even the IrAAC-operated Swiss-made Pilatus PC-7 trainers were deployed on airstrips constructed near the battlefield to fly close air support. These light strikers could carry up to 450 kilograms of ordnance – usually consisting of two gun-pods and two rocket launchers, and lacked sophisticated self defence systems: unsurprisingly, the Iranians soon claimed four of them as shot down.

On 15 March the counter-offensive began with Hayyan's 5th Mechanised Division striking the bridgehead on the west bank of the Tigris with powerful support from both the IrAF and IrAAC (which flew 415 and 320 sorties respectively), destroying the pontoon bridges even though Pasdaran teams used SA-7 MANPADs to bring down several of the helicopters involved. The Iranian hope that Dejkam's Task Force Najaf would pin down the enemy rapidly proved forlorn, while the shortage of artillery ammunition and the extreme range from the North Majnoon batteries meant there was little fire support. The defenders were dreadfully exposed in an area with little cover and with little time to prepare anything but the most rudimentary defences. During the evening the isolated and badly gassed Pasdaran began to give way, and during the night the survivors re-crossed the Tigris.

Some of the IRGC-operated Kashayars (BTR-50s re-engined with US-made diesels) installed ZPU-machineguns on the rear deck of their vehicles, for enhanced air defence. (Tom Cooper Collection)

They were to receive no respite, for at dawn of 16 March the main Iraqi counter-offensive began along the eastern bank of the Tigris as their engineers pumped water from the Tigris into the marshes and bank to flood the Iranian defences. During 16 and 17 March the IrAF launched an all-out effort, flying 800 sorties with every available Sukhoi Su-20, Su-22, MiG-23BN, and even with Mirage F.1EQs (deployed only as interceptors before February 1984). The IrAAC's helicopter gunships flew another 825 sorties. Unsurprisingly, Fakhri's advance made rapid progress: the Guards Division pushed south from the Uzayr area, inflicting heavy casualties and reaching Rashid by the evening, but there the Pasdaran made a stand, leading to a bitter all-night battle before they were driven out in the early morning, allowing the 35th Infantry Division to mop up. Two Task Force Najaf survivors later said:

> The Iraqis had so much artillery that they would pin us in place – then they would unleash wave upon wave of tanks followed by Republican Guard troops who were very well trained, highly motivated and willing to fight us face to face. We lacked the equipment to stop the Guards' tanks who forced us back.[14]

Well dug-in troops of the Iraqi III Corps, in position north of Basra. The soldier in the foreground is manning an RPK-74 light machinegun. (Albert Grandolini Collection)

In addition to overwhelming material strength, Thanun was aided by his superior COMINT capability. From 12 March the IrAF joined the 3rd Wing IrAAC in both CAS and battlefield interdiction sorties flying a total of 767 fixed-wing and 530 rotary-wing sorties by the 14th of the month. The vast majority of these

Sa'adi made slower progress, led by the 6th Armoured Division supported by the Basra Defence Command, which started north-east of Qurnah, and then advanced through the cultivated belt via Khudr towards Uzayr despite desperate resistance from Task Force Karbala. These attacks caused great concern among the defenders; two of the Ali Ibn Abu Talib Division's five remaining battalions took heavy losses and needed to be relieved by battalions of the 28th Division from the Majnoons. Even then, the IRGC's forward positions were on the verge of destruction already by early afternoon. Although having to fight its way across numerous streams, on 18 March the 6th Armoured Division met Fakhri's spearhead at Hamayoun (10 kilometres north-east of Qurnah) as the surviving Pasdaran withdrew into the marshes. The seriousness of the defeat is shown by the loss on the same day of the commander of the Mohammad Rasoolallah Division, Haj Abbas Karimi (his predecessor was killed during Khyber). Here, as in the north, the Iraqis captured numerous boats which they used to help mop up the enemy.[15]

In a desperate and belated attempt to relieve pressure on their colleagues, Rafsanjani and the clerics demanded an attack on South Majnoon from North Majnoon. Already on 18 March, the 3rd Saheb al-Zaman Division was brought down from the Dezful front, and rushed to launch a nocturnal attack in a vain attempt to recover the lost ground. Unsurprisingly, considering all the Iraqi units concentrated in the area, it failed to regain all of the islet, leaving the Iraqis with a toe-hold on South Majnoon. On the night from 20 to 21 March, as three days of rain began, a new attack was made upon two brigades of the 31st Infantry Division, but again the Iraqi defences held. Indeed, the Iranian counter-attack was blasted away to a degree that for all intents and purposes, Operation Badr was over by 23 March.[16]

The lessons learned

Two commentators observed:

> Operation Badr was ambitious, but conceived and executed by amateurs incapable of handling its complexities, especially after the normal frictions of war intervened.[17]

US satellite intelligence estimated a total of 12,000 men from both sides had died, but the Iraqis probably lost 9,000 men including 1,500 prisoners, mostly a battalion of 429th Brigade, while the Iranians probably suffered 17,000 casualties including 3,000 to chemical weapons. Although the IRIA was prepared to participate in the later stages of the operation, and 77th Division received a bridging company from 16th Armoured Division on 12 March, few of its men actively participated in the battle. In turn, 55th Airborne Brigade's strength was reported to have declined following losses during Badr. Material losses were surprisingly low: in the Iranian case because their artillery was never physically threatened, while they deployed little armour; the Iraqis reportedly lost only 45 AFVs and 17 aircraft (including 11 helicopters). However, US intelligence estimated that 260 Iraqi MBTs (a third of their strength) were knocked out by RPGs and recoilless artillery. The IRIAA was extremely active and flew 987 sorties, compared with more than 1,500 from the IrAAC: it launched 23 TOW missiles and evacuated 1,659 wounded, in turn losing 14 helicopters shot down or badly damaged, together with three crewmembers.[18]

The Iraqis, who called this campaign 'The Crown of Battle' (Taj el-Ma'arik), were proud of their achievements in smashing the offensive and in which they had shown determination and resolution, but as usual foreign observers expressed often bitter critique. The British Military Attaché, Colonel R.C. Eccles, probably reflected the views of the other members of the Diplomatic Corps:

> Most observers agree that at face value the resourcefulness and determination shown by the Iranians must have contrasted strongly with an almost incredible degree of Iraqi military incompetence that allowed this to occur.

Eccles concluded that the Iraqi high command under-estimated enemy determination and was surprised by enemy persistence:

> However, the Iraqis quickly assembled an overwhelming counter-attack force, at least two armoured divisions strong, which effectively overran Iranians' positions East and West of the Tigris on about 16 March.

He noted that when the international press corps, who were taken on a tour of the battlefield on 17 March saw evidence of heavy Iraqi casualties in men and machines which:

> suggest that the counter-attacks may have been conducted hastily and with less than perfect all arms coordination, but they were nevertheless successful because of the unequalness of the fight.

US intelligence noted that Badr saw poor levels of combined arms training, with many counter-attacking Iraqi tanks lost to RPGs fired from the side and rear due to the absence of close infantry support.[19]

Yet both sides were surprisingly content with their performances.

Ready to meet a tank-tipped counterattack is this Iranian anti-armour team, armed with a 106mm M40 recoilless gun mounted on a jeep. Although officially a 106mm weapon, this gun actually used 105mm ammunition: the term 106mm was used to avoid confusion in the logistical chain. (Tom Cooper Collection)

The Iranians were now certain they could exploit terrain to balance enemy firepower superiority while surprise remained a key element in their planning. Iranian Chief of Staff Colonel Ismail Sohrabi stated:

> Our blitzes are planned so as to make it hard for the enemy to redeploy its forces to the areas attacked. In our various operations, while we aim to avoid sustaining heavy casualties, we seek to surprise the enemy and to wear him out psychologically...We wish to render it almost impossible for enemy commanders to plan properly; our operations enable our men to fight an enemy with superior hardware.

An Iranian 106mm recoilless gun firing at enemy armour. The biggest drawback of this weapon was the massive back-blast that immediately revealed the weapons' position. Survival of the crew depended on their skill in quickly moving away after firing. (Tom Cooper Collection)

Consequently, the politicians and clerics in Tehran remained confident 'Islamic warfare' was the key to success and while the Pasdaran had been unable to cut the Baghdad-Basra highway they had at least reached it.[20]

But Rezai explained:

> This tactic has not replaced our previous ones. it keeps the enemy constantly entangled. This strengthens our main tactic, which is launching big and determined operations.[21]

The Iraqis too were content although the last shots of Badr had barely been fired before Saddam called a meeting in Baghdad on 25 March so the Defence Minister, the Chief of Staff, corps and arms commanders could review the lessons learned. The active defence policy was confirmed and the corps were ordered to plan more limited attacks and raids to gain or regain terrain which would improve overall defence and boost morale. The investment in the road network had clearly paid off and allowed the Republican Guard to be deployed in force, aided by a large force of tank transporters, and the Guard was now becoming a strategic reserve. In addition Saddam was prepared to loosen the reins slightly on his front line commanders. One decision from the conference was to upgrade the status of the ETOH: this became the VI Corps in the summer of 1985, by when it included the Marshes Command Forces – without the 25th and 35th Infantry Divisions, which were transferred to IV Corps. As compensation the new corps received the 12th Armoured Division, 4th and 25th Infantry Divisions, and – in 1986 – the newly-established 40th Infantry Division.[22]

An extremely exposed Iranian ZU-23 gun engaging an aerial target. This was a towed weapon that was probably rapidly deployed in response to a threat – or the crew felt very confident. (Tom Cooper Collection)

Despite the end of Badr the active defence policy ensured that the marshes continued to echo to the sounds of battle. On 19 March, the 31st Infantry Division and 601st Infantry Brigade staged a raid near South Majnoon and two days later 19th Infantry Division staged the Operation Blessed Days of Victory near the same area. An attack by 28th Infantry Brigade (31st Infantry Division) on 27 June gained more of South Majnoon. The new VI Corps was also in action with 2nd Mountain Brigade striking into the marshes on 17 May to wreck enemy bridges, while between 31 May and 2 July the 4th and 25th Infantry Divisions made spoiling attacks to destroy supplies and boats. This provoked Iranian reaction with Operation Mozzafar on 6 June and Tapper 2 at South Majnoon on 7 June, followed by another raid (Tapper 4) on 21 June, while during the second half of June, the 25th Infantry Division IRGC ran Operation Qods-3, and – on 6 August – Qods-5. Raids and minor offensives continued, principally in the northern and central fronts during the rest of the year, often by battalion or company size units.[23]

To prevent the enemy repeating his attack with greater success the Defence Ministry in Baghdad forwarded a directive from the President's Office on 25 March 1985 demanding the destruction of villages within the marshes and the destruction of both reed beds and palm groves around the edges to strengthen the eastern bank's defences. A committee was established at Uzayr in April to clear the marshes southwards to Qurnah: by the beginning of 1986 at least 21 villages had been razed and some 25,000 people forcibly removed as the Basra-wing of the Ba'ath Party mobilised civilians (including school children) to clear the marshes and the palm groves northeast of Qurnah. A *cordon sanitaire* manned by security police and the Popular Army was then established to prevent infiltrators and deserters, although in January 1987 the Pasdaran moved MRLS teams into the marshes and Baghdad began to plan draining the area. The Iraqi defences were further strengthened by creating earth/sand walls 4.5-6 metres high between the Tigris and the Baghdad-Basrah highway, and by demolishing almost all the villages and individual houses which straddled the highway – especially in the east – to improve fields of fire. In addition they built a new logistic road alongside the Amara-Qurna road, but 15 kilometres further west. Large armoured forces, at least a division, were deployed between the wall and the desert west of the road for a distance of about 20 kilometres north of Qurna.[24]

4
THE THRIVING ARMOURERS

From the opening shots of 'Ramadan' the southern campaigns were dominated by one inescapable fact, Iran was hamstrung by shortages of modern heavy weapons and ammunition which doomed any conventional trial of strength. However hard the Iranians tried to overcome their weakness through attacking in terrain favourable to themselves, ultimately they still faced such a trial and inevitably would lose, indeed throughout this period Iran had only 1,000 MBTs, 1,400 AFVs and 600-800 guns while Iraq had some 3,000 MBTs, 2,500 AFVs and 1,800 guns.

In part this was because Iran was suffering major economic problems with the cost of the war – estimated at US$163.7 billion by March 1984, of which $53.7 billion was lost by the oil industry. Daily oil exports dropped from 1.3 million barrels to 800,000 in the autumn of 1986, while the world glut meant that prices fell from US$36.71 per barrel in 1980 to US$30.20 in 1982. Even though Tehran exceeded its OPEC production quota of 1.2 million barrels a day with an output of 2.3 million barrels a day, revenues from strong currencies were barely sufficient to cover armament procurements. Consequently, the country's internal transport was decimated, domestic flights cancelled and private car owners allowed only 40 litres of fuel per month. Tehran's only external source of funds was President Muammar Gaddafi who also supplied limited quantities of military equipment. In mid-1983 an American intelligence analyst noted: "Tehran remains critically short of tanks, aircraft, artillery ammunition and a steady supply of spare parts necessary to keep its equipment fully operational.'[1]

The Shah's attempts at self-sufficiency were continued through the Defence Industries Organisation (DIO) created in 1983, while the Pasdaran established their own weapons manufacturers from early 1984. However, the Iranian factories largely produced assault rifles, RPGs, mortars and mortar bombs, while there was limited production of four-wheel-drive vehicles, communications and chemical protection equipment. Consequently, there was no solution for Tehran but to look abroad: by 1986 it was importing military equipment worth US$2.2 billion a year and signed further contracts worth US$14 billion (see Table 6 for major orders for ground forces equipment).

During the 1970s, the Shah of Iran had established a domestic armaments industry which the revolutionary regime took-over under

One of the most important additions to the Iraqi arsenal of the mid-1980s, was a batch of Mirage F.1EQ-4 fighter-bombers, the first of which reached Iraq in 1983. Equipped with an advanced navigation/attack system and armament of Western origin, they saw intensive service in counterattacks against Iranian offensives. (Hugues Deguillebon Collection)

One of the major reinforcements for the IrAF acquired in 1984, were the first of an eventual 55 MiG-23ML interceptors. Still not matching the Grumman F-14A Tomcats of the IRIAF, they offered a relatively cheap yet effective performance, combined with armament that was unknown to Iranians. In one of their first combat operations, a pair of Iraqi MiG-23MLs shot down the Tomcat flown by the leading IRIAF tactician of this war, Hashem All-e-Agha, on 11 August 1984. (Tom Cooper Collection)

the umbrella organization of the Defence Industries Organisation (DIO), but this took years to recover from the revolutionary chaos of 1979-1980. The DIO produced many of the small arms, RPGs and mortars but the heaviest weapons which emerged were MRLS, such as the Fajr-3 installed on Japanese-made Isuzu, and then Mercedes, 6x6 trucks. The largest imported weapons included the North Korean-made 240mm M1985 long-range guns. Small arms, mortar bombs, 105mm and 155mm artillery shells were produced too, possibly meeting up to half the requirements in some categories, as were CJ-3B light trucks of Indian design, and gas masks. All of this helped to reduce arms imports. In addition, Iran benefitted from the facilities of Iran Electronics Industries (Sana-ey Electronik-e Iran)

Table 6: Major Arms Orders by Iran 1982-1986

Order Placed	Country	Equipment			Delivered
		Type	Model	Number	
1982	China	MRLS	122mm	100	1982-1987
	China	MRLS	107mm	200	1982-1986
	Syria	MBT	T-55	120	1982
1983	Austria	Towed Arty	155mm	300	1983-1984
	North Korea	Towed Arty	130mm	480	
1984	Argentina	Towed Arty	155mm	10	1984
1985	China	MBT	Type-59	440	1985-1986
	China	Towed Arty	122mm	100	1985-1986
	China	Towed Arty	130mm	100	1985-1986
	China	MRLS	107mm	250	1985-1986
	China	MRLS	122mm	100	1985-1986
	North Korea	MRLS	240mm	100	1985-1990
1986	China	Towed Arty	130mm	120	1987
	USSR	IFV	BMP-1	400	1986-1989
	USSR	APC	BTR-60	400	1986
	Vietnam	MBT	M-48	80	1986-1987
	Vietnam	APC	M-113	200	1986-1987

After a temporary halt in the period 1980-1982, Iraq continued purchasing additional Sukhoi Su-22M-2, Su-22M-3 and Su-22M-4K fighter-bombers, which became something like the "battlewagons" of the IrAF during the war with Iran. This Su-22M was operated by No. 5 Squadron. (Tom Cooper Collection)

In 1984, Iraq received the second batch of 12 Mi-25 helicopter gunships from the Soviet Union. (Farzin Nadimi Collection)

During the mid-1980s, Iraq acquired the final batch of SA.342K Gazelle attack helicopters, armed with HOT ATGMs. (Ali Tobchi Collection)

or IEI established in 1972 which produced the US AN/PRC-77 VHF FM and AN/PRC-105 HF manpack transceiver, and vehicle-based VRC/GRC-105 systems and later developed tactical encryption systems for them.

Nevertheless, Iran – just like Iraq – remained overdependent upon foreign equipment. Living in the rarefied world of religious mania the clerics and their supporters had succeeded in isolating Iran from its potential western sources of military equipment and, reflecting the growing economic importance of the Pacific Rim, were forced to turn to the Far East and especially China and North Korea. In 1982, Tehran received the first deliveries under a US$1.5 billion defence contract from China; this included armour, artillery (tube and rocket), infantry weapons, missiles, ammunition and tank engines. Another contract with China followed in 1985: worth some US$3.1 billion, it resulted in deliveries of a similar range of equipment: Beijing is known to have supplied some Type-69 MBTs – derivatives of the Soviet T-54 with a 100mm rifled gun – but Iran appears to have purchased no tank transporters or heavy equipment transporters (HETs) for these.[2] The towed artillery supplied was also often a derivative or development of the Soviet systems and included the Type-83 122mm howitzer, the Type-59 130mm gun (M-46) and Type-81 truck-mounted 122mm MRLS (BM-21). The Type-63 towed 107mm MRLS, however, was a Chinese weapon and was the backbone of Pasdaran divisional fire-support battalions. Later on, the Chinese contracts included 'big ticket' items – such as combat aircraft and associated weapons, long range surface-to-air and coastal-defence missile systems. The ground forces did receive significant quantities of missile systems, including – starting from 1982 – 6,500

Hongjian (Red Arrow) 73 – or HJ-73 – anti-armour missiles from the first contract and 500 HN-5 MANPADS (Chinese copy of the SA-7) ordered in 1985. Between 1982 and 1985, North Korea is estimated to have supplied artillery, infantry weapons, missiles and ammunition worth US$510. The Soviet Union launched another attempt at rapprochement with Iran in 1986, and this effort resulted in sale of some surplus or second-hand troop carriers, about 100 SA-7 launchers and 400 missiles, but also some ammunition and spares. Up to 2,000 Soviet-made 9K11 Malyutka ATGMs (ASCC/NATO-code AT-3 'Sagger') were delivered by Syria from 1982 and an order to North Korea saw another 4,000 delivered from 1986 until after the war. Syria and Libya provided some heavy weapons but mostly supplied infantry weapons, both individual and crew-served, as well as ammunition; their aircraft joining those of the IRIAF to fly equipment into Tabriz airbase. Eventually, between 1980 and 1987, Moscow is estimated to have provided military equipment and ammunition worth US$11.8 billion to Tehran, including a licence to manufacture AK-47 assault rifles. Even so, Iraq remained preferred Soviet client in the region.[3]

China and North Korea also assisted Iran to purchase material covertly in the commercial market apparently under the 'Dermavand' Project, named after Iran's highest mountain. Necessary funding was channelled in 1985 and 1986 through the Belgian Banque Lambert. These arrangements met some of Iran's requirements but there were routinely 100% mark-ups, and a single much-prized TOW anti-armour missile worth US$5,500 was sold at US$60,000 to Tehran, while deliveries were irregular and neither quantity nor quality could be guaranteed. Still, such business remained extremely lucrative and thus went on; in 1985 Tehran spent US$100 million with Arab and Swiss dealers to regain captured equipment including M48 MBTs, the dealers earning at least a US$10 million commission. Around the same time, a Syrian attempt to acquire Belgian made self-propelled 155mm howitzers failed when the vendor demanded US$1 million per gun!

Heavy weapons were the most difficult to acquire. In 1983, a US$440 million contract was placed with the Austrian state-owned company Noricum for 300 GHN-45 155mm howitzers. About

Further diversifying its sources of arms (in order to prevent any possible arms embargos), Iraq acquired three batches including a total of 75 Messerschmitt-Bölkow-Blohm (MBB) Bo.105 attack helicopters, and then a batch of 16 Japanese-built BK.117B-1 helicopters (developed in cooperation with Germany), one of which is visible in this photograph. The first of the BK.117B-1s arrived in September 1987. They were primarily used for VIP-transport and search and rescue purposes. (Ali Tobchi Collection)

Another, perhaps unexpected addition to the IrAAC came from the USA, in the form of 60 McDonnell Douglas MD.500 Defender helicopters. Ostensibly sold for civilian purposes, all saw extensive combat service during the war with Iran, often in combination with Mi-25s. (Farzin Nadimi Collection)

100 of these weapons appear to have been delivered via Libya, but a year after the war ended the Austrian government decided to divest itself of the company. Iran also acquired some Swiss-made Oerlikon twin 35mm AA guns, but these were primarily used to bolster the air defences of the strategically important oil-exporting terminal at Khark Island. US authorities sought to curtail this trade and in November 1985 completed a 'sting' operation which prevented the clandestine shipment to Iran of a huge shipment including 18 F-4s, 46 A-4s, 13 F-5s, and bombs, anti-armour missiles and radars which might have tipped the scales in the Faw Peninsula.[4] Officially at least, most United Nations members respected the arms embargos imposed upon Iran and Iraq already in September

Another new weapon system acquired by Iraq in the mid-1980s was the Brazilian-made Astros II (an acronym for Artillery Saturation Rocket System), about 60 of which were delivered starting from 1983. Each battery had four AV-LMU launch-vehicles and two AV-RMD transport vehicles, and an AV-VCC fire-control vehicle with Contraves Fieldguard radar. Also known as SS-40, the launch-vehicle had 16 tubes that fired 152kg rockets out to a maximum range of 35 kilometres. (Tom Cooper Collection)

Although spreading rumours that the IRIAF was non-operational and grounded, the Iraqis knew that the Iranian air force was hitting back at every opportunity. Correspondingly, Baghdad continued purchasing SAMs throughout the war, eventually acquiring over 18,000 different rounds during the 1980s. This is a launch vehicle for the Soviet-made 2K12 Kub (SA-6 Gainful) medium range system. (Joav Efrati Collection)

1980. Unofficially, it was anything but the case: the embargo was simply ignored, often with at least some degree of government support. Iranian oil was widely used to lubricate deals, with such US-allies as Singapore, South Korea and Taiwan willing to provide spares for US-built vehicles and aircraft. Some nations, notably Brazil and France, were willing to supply both sides. During 1984 an Iranian delegation visited Brazil and sought equipment from the aerospace industry and MRLS. Brasilia first granted permission for deliveries of Embraer EMB.312 Tucano training aircraft but then banned exports to Tehran. The Iranians then initiated attempts to acquire Brazilian equipment through Libya which attempted to acquire EE-9 Cascavel armoured cars and EE-11 Urutu APCs – together with spares for them and ammunition for the 90mm guns – but, the Brazilian Foreign Ministry blocked these efforts for fear of compromising even more lucrative sales to Iraq.

This contrasted with the US$120 million worth of equipment, including electronic components, supplied by France to Iran from 1983-1987 – at least according to US intelligence reports. The majority of this included 450,000 155mm and 203mm artillery shells, delivered by GIAT – partially via Cherbourg and Zaventem in Belgium, partially via French company Minerve via Saudi Arabia – with false end-user certificates (the latter declared them as ordered by Brazil, Portugal, Thailand and Yugoslavia), in an enterprise that lasted until several months after the end of war. In addition the French company SNPE supplied Iran with explosives in an enterprise stopped by Paris in March 1986. During the same year, Italian subsidiaries of the French company Luchaire – Consar and S.E.A. – reportedly supplied Iran with ammunition, too.

Italian sales of military equipment to Iran totalled at about US$350 million in 1983 and US$200 million in 1986. Reportedly, they included 36 OTO Melara 105mm mountain howitzers, Borletti fuzes, 92 Oerlikon Italiana anti-aircraft guns, Marconi Italiana and Selenia radars, Valsella Meccanotecnica SpA land mines and 1,400 Luigi Franchi sights. Late in 1986 Rome's Trade Minister, Mr Rino Formica, confirmed his ministry continued to approve these sales because, he claimed, the government never officially informed him of an arms embargo!

Other European governments were at least as happy to turn a blind eye to the UN-imposed arms embargo. Spain supplied US$280 million worth of ammunition – mostly mortar bombs but also some recoilless artillery – through Syria and Libya until May 1986, and Portugal's Spel did so from 1984 until 1987. Dutch company Muiden Chemie reportedly supplied Iran with US$100 million worth of ammunition from 1984-1987 (all delivered via Austria, Portugal and Yugoslavia), while in 1984 German customs seized 200 tonnes of explosives produced by Sweden's Dynamit

Nobel and allegedly destined for Iran via Yugoslavia.

Small arms and ammunition reached Iran from Argentina (which supplied US$31 million worth of equipment), Bulgaria, Cuba, Czechoslovakia, Gabon, Greece, Pakistan, Portugal, South Korea, and Nicaragua but many countries also helped the Iranian war machine in other ways. Greece supplied Continental Teledyne engines for M48 and M60 MBTs, Turkey supplied communications equipment, while Singapore illegally sold some 200 Swedish Bofors RBS-70 MANPADS worth US$307 million and also arranged for the delivery of 20mm Oerlikon naval guns. South Korea provided spares while Vietnam provided both spares, AFVs, and even a batch of second-hand Northrop F-5E/B and F-5E fighter-bombers in a US$400 million deal agreed in July 1986.

Tehran also benefitted from dual-use equipment, especially vehicles which were ostensibly for civilian use. East and West Germany, South Korea and Japan were major suppliers while India and Sweden each provided 200 trucks, Yugoslavia 500 trucks (including 30 heavy-load vehicles) in 1983 alone. The United Kingdom sold some US$200 million worth of vehicles to Iran, including 3,000 Land Rovers, as Whitehall desperately wriggled to find some way of cashing in on the booming market. During 1985 some US$130 million worth of spares for British-designed AFVs were flown to Tehran and eventually six radars worth US$380 million were sold for 'air traffic control' to replace US-made sensors.

A vast stock of US equipment, worth US$12.2 billion according to Tehran and US$9.9 billion according to Washington – which had been paid for by the Shah before 1979 – remained tantalisingly beyond reach of Tehran. This included M113 APCs, air defence weapons and electronics – and spares for virtually everything. In 1979 Washington offered to buy back this material but Tehran refused and by December 1986 the Americans reported most of the equipment had deteriorated and was useless. A year after the war ended Tehran began moves to recover this cornucopia and in December 1991 the Iran-United States Claims Tribunal in the Hague saw Washington agree to pay Iran US$278 million for defence equipment impounded after Iranian 'students' took US Embassy staff hostage. During the negotiations the tribunal had helped arrange the two sides would pay US$2.3 billion to meet each others' claims, but in 1998 Tehran asked the International Court of Justice to consider its claim that by ending the Foreign Military Sales (FMS) programme to Iran in 1979, Washington should pay US$10 billion in compensation for excessive payments, failure to deliver equipment, unserviceable equipment delivered and storage fees for material in the United States.

That was at least the official side of relations between Iran and the USA. Unofficially, the United States – or 'The Great Satan' – were selling weapons to Tehran all the time between 1980 and 1983, foremost via Israel: reportedly, the latter had supplied US$3.2 billion worth of military equipment – including aircraft spare parts, mortars and ammunition for 105mm tank guns and mortars – to Iran during the same period. The USA became involved with Iran again during the desperate effort to regain influence and free some of hostages taken by Hezbollah in Lebanon during the infamous Iran-Contra deal (which saw the resulting profit being diverted to support the anti-Communist Nicaraguan Contras). Much of what reached Iran was at least officially declared as 'beyond the shelf life', and again was delivered via Israel. The system worked so that Israel would sell its surplus stocks of older weapons, which in turn would be replaced by deliveries of newly-manufactured weapons from the USA. For example, between August 1985 and November 1986, Iran supposedly received 2,008 BGM-71A TOW ATGMs and 238 MIM-23B I-HAWK SAMs in this fashion: unofficial Iranian sources confirmed the delivery of 'about 2,000' TOWs, but stressed that all the HAWK SAMs were older MIM-23A which the IRIAF couldn't use. Similarly while the CIA requested 4,342 individual items for Iranian I-HAWKs only 3,976, worth US$4.3 million, were actually dispatched. Although these supplies were not on the scale which Tehran had hoped for they undoubtedly helped Iranian forces.[5]

In February 1987 the New York Times published details of alleged US involvement in the 'Damavand' Project and claimed that Washington was aware by early 1984 of efforts by private contractors to supply 39 F-4E Phantoms, 25 AH-1 Cobras, air- and ship-launched missiles together with 150 M48A5 tanks, 50,000 M16A1 rifles and artillery fire control computers. Reportedly funded via Cairo – certainly the closest Iraqi ally of the time – this deal was actually never realized.

By contrast, Iraq had almost uninterrupted access to foreign arms producers although – due to the almost complete destruction of its oil industry by the IRIAF early during the war – Baghdad's economy faced incredible difficulties paying for equipment in the long term.

The longer the war with Iran lasted, the bigger emphasis Iraqis put upon reinforcing their artillery units, until these outclassed the Iranians. The primary divisional guns remained Soviet-designed 122mm howitzers and 130mm guns. The latter were usually available in the form of M-46 guns, one of which can be seen here. They could fire up to six shells, weighing 33kg each, per minute over a range of 27 kilometres. (Albert Grandolini Collection)

An Iranian mechanized battle group including Scorpion reconnaissance tanks, M60 MBTs and even one 155mm self-propelled howitzer. Such massive formations became a rarity during the mid-1980s, because the Iraqi Air Force established air supremacy over the battlefield. (Tom Cooper Collection)

Saddam's bitter enemy, President Assad, cut Iraq's oil pipeline through his country and with his pipelines to Turkey harassed by Kurdish guerrillas, daily oil exports dropped from a pre-war 1.3 billion barrels to 700,000 barrels: this was barely enough to sustain the country, never mind a war. A second pipeline to Turkey was built and when it became operational in 1984 it brought exports to 1 billion barrels a day. However, even after the CIA estimated that the Iraqi oil exports were back to US$2.3 billion, a year later, Baghdad was spending about 245% of its oil revenues on imports of military equipment. The reason for this absurdity was simple: since late 1981, bankrupt Iraq was saved by lavishly borrowing money – foremost from Kuwait, but from Saudi Arabia, too.

When the war broke out Baghdad had foreign exchange reserves worth US$40 billion. These were quickly depleted and by 1986 down to US$5 billion. Thus, already in 1981 Kuwait City and Riyadh arranged a set of loans totalling US$12 billion, followed by another US$5.5 billion in 1982. By 1986 Iraq had received US$30-50 billion worth of largesse, before the 'Oil Shock' of that year strained the economies of Gulf states to cut back. Furthermore, not only Kuwait and Saudi Arabia, but especially Jordan, all provided safe harbours into which military supplies for Iraq were transported – sometimes by ships organized into outright convoys, usually with official convoys too. Multiple European trucking companies earned handsome profits from organising the transhipment of the contraband from ports like that in Aqaba (Jordan) to Baghdad, during the 1980s.

Indeed, despite the de-facto bankruptcy of Iraq, Saddam's prolificacy of spending continued unchecked and from 1981-1986 the country placed orders for arms worth US$32. Annual imports of military-related equipment grew from US$4.3 billion in 1982 to US$7.7 billion in 1986, turning Iraq into the World's biggest arms importer (major acquisitions of ground-forces-related equipment are listed in Table 7). According to US intelligence, the largest supplier was the USSR, which received contracts worth US$12.4 billion – most of that for combat aircraft and missiles – and was followed by France with contracts related just to Mirage F.1EQ fighter-bombers reaching staggering US$6 billion (those for other equipment added about US$3.8 billion), China with contracts worth US$3.9 billion, and Brazil (US$1.2 billion).

Some of this largesse was not as generous as it appeared; most of the Soviet T-62 MBTs were surplus vehicles which arrived after extensive use with the Soviet Army. The Soviet-designed MBTs were very much lower in quality compared with those of western manufacturers and the Iraqis sought to incorporate western technology to improve them, or at least acquire MBTs of Czechoslovak or Polish origin, which were considered as of better quality. While T-62s had infra-red searchlights for night operations they lacked laser rangefinders which first appeared in T-72s delivered from early 1983. French laser rangefinders were acquired and fitted into T-55 MBTs: without the addition of a fire control computer this was of limited effect. Appliqué spaced armour was added to T-55s (and also to BMP-1s), to reduce the effect of shaped charges, initially in commanders' vehicles and then generally applied.

There are many contemporary reports of British Chieftains being used by the Iraqis and even of Kuwait supplying Baghdad from its own inventory. Whitehall was certainly willing to provide Chieftain and its FV4030 derivatives to Baghdad ostensibly through a Jordanian contract, but the Iraqis were all too well aware of the vehicle's limitations and preferred the superior T-72, although there were negotiations with a view to an Iraqi purchase of what would be Challenger I with Chobham armour. However, a combination of the British reluctance to supply arms to a country at war, and Iraqi bankruptcy, as well as concern that the arms might be compromised through the Iraqis letting their Soviet allies take a closer look, resulted in related negotiations of 1982-1983 period remaining fruitless.

While China supplied MBTs including a derivative of the T-55, the Type-69-I with 100mm smoothbore gun, together with 122mm

Table 7: Major Arms Orders by Iraq 1982-1986

Order Placed	Country	Equipment			Delivered
		Type	Model	Number	
1982	China	MBT	Type-69	1500	1983-1987
	China	Towed Arty	122mm	200	1983-1986
	China	Towed Arty	152mm	200	1983-1986
	France	APC	M-3-VTT	115	1983-1984
	Poland	MBT	T-72	250	1982-1990
	USSR	MRLS	122mm	200	1983-1984
	USSR	Towed Arty	122mm	576	1982-1988
	Poland	APC	MT-LB	750	1983-1990
1983	China	MRLS	107mm	100	1984-1988
	Poland	APC	MT-LB	750	1983-1984
	USSR	Recon	PT-76	200	1984
	USSR	SP Mortar	240mm 2S4	10	1983
	USSR	MRLS	BM-21	200	1983-1984
1984	Egypt	Towed Arty	122mm	120	1985-1988
	Romania	MBT	TR-77	150	1985-1987
	South Africa	Towed Arty	155mm	200	1985-1986
	USSR	Recon	PT-76	200	1984
1985	Egypt	Towed Arty	122mm	210	1985-1989
	USSR	MRLS	122mm	360	1986-1988
1986	USSR	SP Arty	Akatsiya	100	1986-1988
	USSR	SP Arty	Gvozdika	100	1987-1989
	USSR	Towed Arty	152	180	1986-1988
	Yugoslavia	MRLS	262mm	2	1987

Type-60 guns as well as Type-83 howitzers, Type-59 130mm guns and the USSR towed D-30 122mm howitzers, neither appears to have provided heavier towed tubes until 1986 when Moscow provided 2A36 Giatsint (Hyacinth) 152mm towed guns together with a second batches of 2S3 Akatsiya 152mm and 2S1 Gvozdika 122mm self-propelled howitzers. For heavier towed tubes the Iraqis turned to western manufacturers and in June 1985 they witnessed a demonstration by France's GIAT of the 155TR towed 155mm howitzer. Unfortunately, while the weapon was demonstrating a high rate of fire with full charges a howitzer exploded and a French non-commissioned officer was killed. Consequently, Baghdad became interested in the Canadian-designed 45-calibre GC-45: already in 1981, an order had been placed for 200 Austria-manufactured GHN-45 howitzers based on this design, and in 1984 an order for a similar number of the South African version manufactured by Denel was placed. Compared with the Soviet D-1 152mm in the Iraqi Army and the US M114 155mm weapon in the IRIA, whose muzzle velocities were 508m/s and 563 m/s, these weapons featured a muzzle velocity of 897 m/s which gave them a range of 29.9 kilometres with Extended Range Full Bore (ERFB) ammunition or 39.6 kilometres with the base-bleed version which were especially hard on barrels. These weapons actually outranged the Coalition field artillery during Operation Desert Storm in 1991. The downside of the situation was that their high performance meant shorter barrel lives. Just as aircraft life is measured in flying hours so gun-barrel life is measured in terms of the number of times it may be fired with the largest number (full charge) of propellant bags or Effective Full Charge (EFC): as of the 1980s, a typical 155mm 52 calibre barrel had a life of 750 EFC while 39 calibre weapons had a life of 2,650 EFC. Guns rarely used full charges but even with limited charges as a projectile moved along the barrel it caused friction on the rifling which was gradually smoothed and made the projectiles less accurate. Tank gun barrels have similar restraints with wear depending upon the type of ammunition used: the 105mm M68 used in IRIA M48s and M60A1s having a life of some 300 EFC with the highest performing anti-armour rounds.[6] The Iraqi Army used huge amounts of artillery ammunition, with the daily rate equivalent to the US Army's weekly rate from World War II. This went so far that while it had depots capable of storing up to 300,000 tonnes of ammunition, it suffered periodic shortages.[7] The prime suppliers were Austria, Belgium, Brazil, China, Czechoslovakia, Egypt, France, Greece, Poland, Jordan, Kuwait, South Africa and the USSR. Eventually, even France's Luchaire and Belgium's PRB began supplying 130mm base-bleed shells for Soviet-made guns. Such was the insatiable demand for ammunition that Baghdad asked Italy's Difesa e Spazio if they could supply ammunition for which they did not have a licence! However, with guns from so many sources and with widely differing ballistic performance it was not only difficult to ensure sustained supplies of rounds and charges, but also difficult to organize fire plans, although fire direction computers reportedly reached some batteries by 1985. There were also problems training gun crews and the Iraqis often had to write in Arabic above Russian, Chinese or English language data plates, and these problems were probably shared with Iranian gunners. Unsurprisingly, as the war

Because of dwindling stocks of BGM-71 TOW missiles, the IRIAA arrived at the idea to mate US-made AGM-65A Maverick guided air-to-surface missiles – actually used by IRIAF F-4Es – to some of its AH-1Js. Here is seen a close-up photograph of such a modification. (Farzin Nadimi Collection)

went on without an end, the Iraqi Army eventually arrived at the decision to start replacing its worn-out artillery pieces instead of just replacing worn-out gun barrels.[8]

The shortage of heavy artillery meant a greater reliance upon MRLS – mostly of Soviet or Chinese origin. Furthermore, a US$600 million contract was placed with Avibras Aeroespacial for 60 SS-40 Astros II MRLS and the first instalment helped to complete development of these weapons. Deliveries began in March 1984 and were completed in 1987 with batteries consisting of four launcher vehicles, a fire control vehicle with Contraves Fieldguard radar and two vehicles to transport spare rockets, with the initial consignment being for 10,000 rockets. In 1986 there was reportedly a US$2 billion contract with Avibras and Engesa for 300 EE-T1 Osario MBTs, 300 EE-9 Cascavael with 90mm and 25mm guns and more Astros II systems including 50-60 of the longer range SS-300 rockets. While the MBTs and some of the other equipment would not be delivered, the contract meant that Iraq would be Brazil's biggest export market, and ammunition sales also proved lucrative for both Chile, Portugal and Spain.

Missile orders were also placed with the trend to acquire basic weapons from the Far East and sophisticated ones from the USSR. In 1985 North Korea received an order for 4,000 of the Susong-Po anti-armour missile, a version of AT-3 Sagger, while the following year China received an order for 1,000 Hong Ying (Red Tassel) 5 or HN-5A MANPADS, a reverse-engineered version of the SA-7. Also in 1986, the USSR received a contract for 3,000 9K111 (ASCC/NATO-code 'AT-4 Spigot') ATGMs comparable with the European Milan system.

In addition to 'big ticket' items, Iraq also received valuable other material. In 1983 an order was placed for 42 LMT Rasit battlefield-surveillance radars in France. Another 18 were ordered in 1986 while the following year 10 Thorni-EMI Cymbeline counter-battery radars were ordered and delivered into 1990. Iraq would buy up to 40% of France's military exports including legitimate dual-use equipment such as Renault TRM-1000 trucks, while Baghdad also received German Daimler Benz and British Land Rovers together with Saboteur Trooper Mk IV all-terrain transports. Some Laird Centaur half-tracks, based upon the Land Rover chassis, were also supplied but the Iraqis wanted associated mine-laying systems which the British refused to supply.

Land mines were supplied to both sides in incredible numbers, Iran having 2.5 million including its pre-war stocks of American ordnance, while Iraq received some 6 million, of which 75% were anti-personnel types costing as little as US$10.00. These, used extensively in the southern battlefield, were mainly from Italy's Valsella, BPD Difesa e Spazio and Tecnovar, who were the lead producers of plastic-bodied ordnance of the 1980s. Chile, China, Egypt and the Soviet Union also supplied mines, although the Chinese ordnance were copies of Soviet designs, while Iraq produced the Valmara 69 anti-personnel mine under licence.

Iraq produced limited quantities of small arms, light and medium mortars, together with RPGs. There were also shell-filling plants as well as factories organized by Thomson-CSF to produce the company's communications equipment, and repair depots at national level for 'hard-' and 'soft'-skinned vehicles as well as MBTs. From 1982 chemical weapon production began and by the end of the war Iraq was said to have produced 3,000 tonnes of chemical agents which filled 100,000 bombs, shells and rocket warheads, as well as some missile warheads. Initially the agents consisted of a crude mustard gas (Bis(2-chloroethyl)sulphide) based upon crude sulphur agents, rather than more lethal sesqui and nitrogen agents. Later the Iraqis began to develop nerve agents, such as Sarin and Tabun, which are organophosphates originally developed as pesticides. As a result of a report by a United Nations investigative mission in April 1984 the United States and the United Kingdom banned the export of chloroethanol, dimethyl-methyl-phosphate, dimethylamine, methyl-phosphonyl-dichloride, methyl-phosphonyl-difluoride, phosphorus-oxychloride, potassium fluoride and thiodiglycol. However, like trucks, many chemical components, had both medical and military usage and could be legitimately exported to Iraq.

5
THE BRILLIANT BLOW

The New Year opened, like 1985, with another Iraqi 'active defence' operation in South Majnoon. Saddam was anxious to regain the island and during the rainy season his engineers used dozens of bulldozers, much earthmoving equipment and hundreds of trucks to drain the island's approaches and to build roads leading into the Fish Lake Line around the Ghuzail.

The Iranians could not help but to be aware of this activity, but Rashid decided to strike before the end of the rainy season when the enemy might expect an attack to exploit the dried ground. The task was assigned to 31st Infantry Division ('al-Hussein Force') under Brigadier Yalcheen Omar Abdil and delegated to Lieutenant Colonel Ibrahim Idwan Abib's 28th Infantry Brigade and Colonel Sami Abbas Mujwil al-Rawi's 49th Infantry Brigade, and the attack date was set by Saddam as Army Day, 6 January 1986.

The attack went in on schedule at 0420 hrs and achieved complete surprise with massive firepower and strong air support, including not only gunships but also some of the new Su-25K 'Frogfoot' attack aircraft. The Iraqis stormed forward exploiting water channels as well as bunds to recapture up to half the island in less than two hours, and claimed to have inflicted 4,000 casualties while they suffered minimal losses.[1]

Planning for a new dawn

Iraqi General Headquarters may have had a secondary motive, to draw the enemy into a bloody battle of attrition for South Majnoon but history repeated itself and the Iranians did not respond. Yet they were not idle and were quietly assembling substantial forces in Khuzestan during the latter half of 1985 as Tehran contemplated its most ambitious offensive at a time when it also faced a major dilemma.

The SDC remained convinced time was on its side and that, like the Union in the American Civil War, it would eventually stretch the enemy to breaking point and had already come tantalisingly close to success in Khyber and 'Badr.' But while Iran had a much larger population than its neighbour it could deploy far fewer men, about a million, which was inadequate to achieve overwhelming numerical superiority over the 800,000-man Iraqi Army. The heavy casualties suffered by Iranian forces and the Iraqis' qualitative superiority exacerbated the problem. By the beginning of 1986 Baghdad and Tehran had 4,500 and 1,000 MBTs respectively while in artillery the figures were 5,000 to 800.[2]

Iraq achieved this largely from gifts and loans provided by Saudi Arabia and the Gulf oil producers, notably Kuwait, as well as limited sales of oil through Turkey. Tehran could still export its oil by sea but its indignation against the Gulf States was increased by what it regarded as their participation in an 'oil conspiracy' to drive down the price of oil by increasing production. With Iran's economy undermined, demands for action grew louder in Tehran, but rather than add to their foes the SDC decided to apply indirect pressure. The Kuwaitis and Saudis were not just bankrolling the Iraqis but also facilitating the movement of arms and equipment. The British Foreign Office, for example, was informed that 110 Chinese tanks

Led by blue-jacketed men – probably Naval Pasdaran of the 104th Emir al-Mu'minin or the 105th al-Kawthar Brigade – a column of Iranian troops moves past a column of vehicles to embark for crossing the Shatt (called the Arvand Road by Iranians), to open Operation Valfajr-8. (Tom Cooper Collection)

Iranian SBS commandos not only ran careful reconnaissance operations of the Faw Peninsula prior to start of Operation Valfajr-8, but also lead the opening attack of this offensive. This photograph shows them in front of one of 20 Agusta-Sikorsky AS.61A-4 Sea Kings, which were sometimes also used for their insertion behind enemy lines. (Farzin Nadimi Collection)

An Iranian Pasdaran commando posing with a Kalashnikov assault rifle in his hand in front of a rush-covered shore. Swimming in the swiftly-moving Shatt proved extremely exhausting for combat divers, while a shortage of wet suits restricted their reconnaissance missions. (Tom Cooper Collection)

later explained the SDC's motives:

Faw was important to us for a number of reasons: First, because with the capture of Faw, Iraq would lose its ability to use the sea, unless they could sneak a boat through Khowr Abdullah (Khawr Abd Allah also Khur Abdollah) under the cover of night. But they would no longer have a military presence in the sea. In addition to that, Iraq no longer could make use of its two oil terminals south of Faw: the al-Amayah and the al-Bakr [sic] oil terminals.

He would later claim that, bearing in mind Khomeini's strict demands for minimum Iraqi civilian casualties, this was an ideal theatre because there were so few civilians.[5]

This was a disingenuous explanation because both oil terminals had been badly damaged by Iranian artillery fire and largely abandoned, while Iranian surface-to-surface missiles were directed at Iraqi cities just as Iraqi missiles struck Iranian cities.[6] Moreover, Iran's control of the Straits of Hormuz stopped Iraqi shipping reaching Umm Qasr (also 'Um Qasir' or 'Om ol-Qasr') which had almost ceased to function as a port. It remained the Iraqi Navy's base, although it posed only a minor threat, and of two-dozen missile- and torpedo-equipped fast attack craft, about half had been sunk or were de-commissioned. By establishing a military presence on the peninsula Iran was clearly demonstrating it could invade Kuwait, which is separated only by the narrow (2 kilometre) Khowr Abdullah from Umm Qasr, and 'persuade' it to abandon the 'oil conspiracy' with the bonus that success would open a new front to Basra. Long after the offensive began, on 23 and 25 February, the Iranians would claim their offensive was designed both to end the interdiction of shipping into Bandar-e Imam Khomeini and Bandar-e Mashur and also to prevent the enemy shelling Khorammshahr and Abadan.

Both Rezai and his clerical supporters in the Pasdaran continued to grow in confidence and they would again spearhead the operation, with training beginning about September 1985. They were slowly learning the lessons from each campaign, like the Allied generals in the First World War and at similar terrible cost. The lessons were dissimilated among the Pasdaran formations, which also received more rigorous combat training, while co-ordination with the IRIA was improved at the Forward Operational Headquarters. Like the troops of English general Oliver Cromwell, the Pasdaran put their trust in God but kept their powder dry. Yet there still remained a chasm of ignorance between the front line troops, including the Pasdaran, and their political and religious masters. Early in 1986 some 8,000 commanders from division to company level were summoned to Tehran to discuss the war because the leaders at the operational level

and 20-30 APC were seen moving northwards through Kuwait from Saudi Arabia on 5 March 1983, while on 12 April a convoy of transporters with 400 new Chinese tanks were seen heading towards Basra.[3]

In the mid or late summer of 1985 Tehran decided to cut the Gordian Knot by seizing the al-Faw (also al-Fao or al-Fawr) Peninsula, which lay along Kuwait's northern border and was only 300 to 1,000 metres across the Shatt al Arab from Iran.[4] Rafsanjani

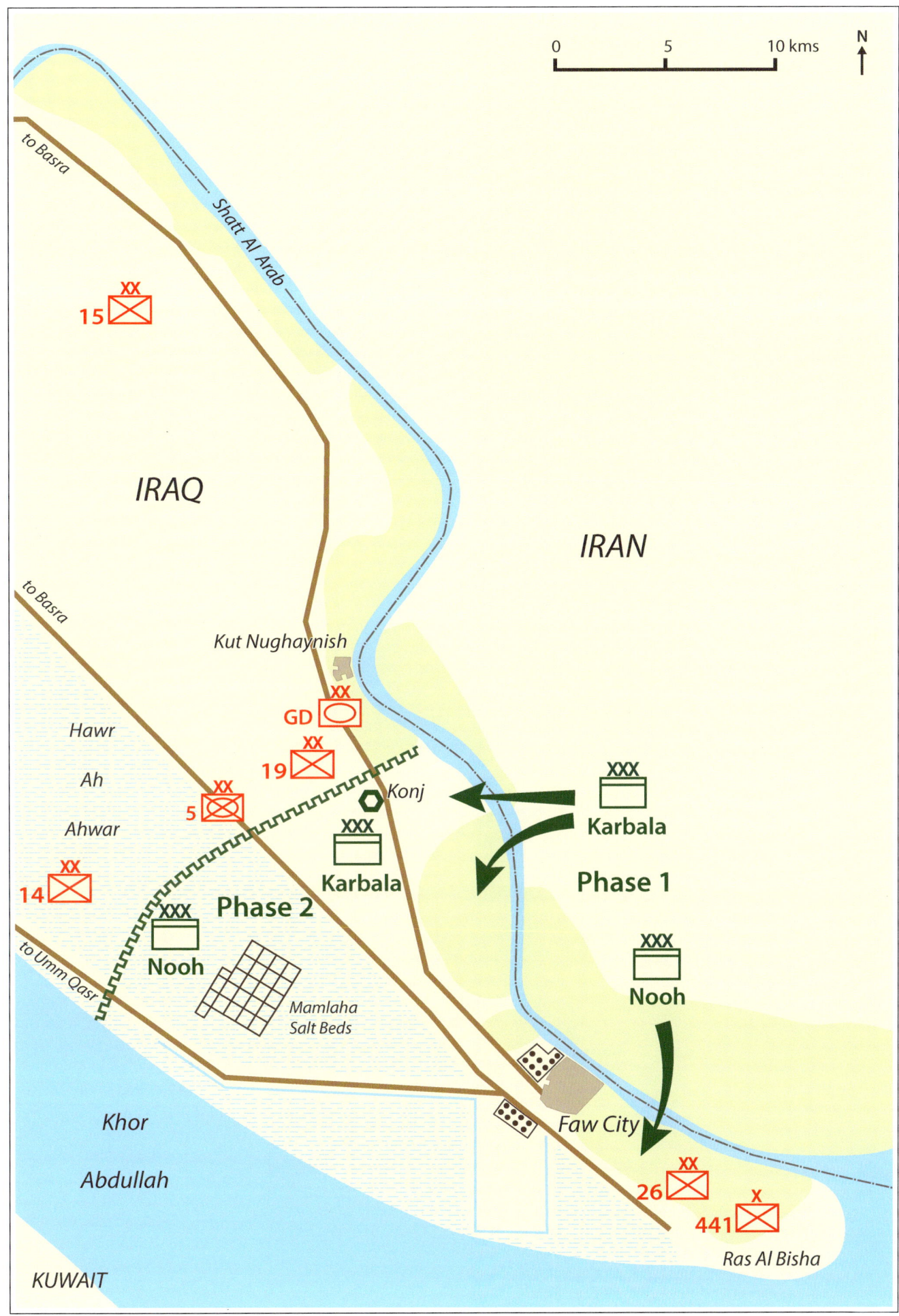

Map 6: The Faw battlefield (Valfajr 8)

Boat crews of the Naval Brigade of the IRGC preparing their craft to carry men and supplies across the Shatt. This photograph was taken in one of the ports east of the battlefield, where flotillas of such boats were gathering. In the background is a Japanese-built Iran Arya class tank landing ship, which was too big to be assigned for this mission. (Tom Cooper Collection)

Abandoned Iraqi defences on the Faw Peninsula. In the background is the rusting hulk of one of dozens of merchantmen trapped inside the waterway at the start of the war, and meanwhile abandoned by its crew. (Tom Cooper Collection)

The Iranians captured a number of armoured fighting vehicles – reportedly including up to 30 MBTs – during their initial advance on the Faw Peninsula. Most belonged to the ill-fated 26th Division. T-54/-55s like this were quickly turned against their former owners. (Tom Cooper Collection)

were unable to make the government and clerics comprehend the front line situation. They had difficulty drafting and executing plans because the objectives and assigned formations would be changed almost at a whim and there appeared no overall strategic blueprint.

There also remained a severe shortage of heavy equipment, much of which had been lost during the battles around the marshes – together with experienced IRIA personnel. The Pasdaran could improve infantry training but even Chinese and North Korean imports could not meet Tehran's requirements for heavy equipment, while a shortage of spares restricted the use of captured equipment, including MBTs for which there were no replacement engines. Despite improved supplies it was impossible to substantially expand either the IRIA or the Pasdaran, and by early 1986 perhaps half the former and two thirds of the latter were truly combat ready.

The clerics decided they needed a professional soldier in charge and they assigned the task to a Khomeini loyalist, 45-year-old Colonel Hassani-Sa'di, whose joint IRIA-Pasdaran Task Force Karbala had played a major role in Badr and would now play a role in the new offensive. For this and its support operations huge numbers of men were mobilised: one report claims half the IRIA and two-thirds of the Pasdaran – although this may be an exaggeration – while 1,000-strong commando battalions were established, too. The demands of the rural economy again meant the new operation would have fewer Basiji, most probably drawn from marsh or coastal villages, and with the well of manpower almost exhausted, from October 1985 women began to be used for rear-area military tasks, and there were plans to send civil servants up to the front. The operation was code-named Valfajr-8 ('Dawn 8') and preparations began in the late summer of 1985 with major amphibious exercises in the Caspian Sea.

The code name 'Valfajr' had previously been used exclusively on the Northern and Central Fronts and was part of the deception programme including attempts to attract enemy attention north of Basra. Like Arras in 1917, the wrecked cities of Khorammshahr and Abadan provided excellent cover for assembling much of the assault force, while the numerous coastal date palm groves along the banks of the Shatt, especially near the mouth, allowed boarding points for men and vehicles, and concealed carefully camouflaged pontoon bridging materials. Because the main attack would be launched from the marshes and wetlands of the northern bank of the Shatt al Arab, the road network south of Abadan between the River Bahmanshir and the Shatt, mostly on bunds, required considerable extension by IRIA engineers, the Pasdaran 44th 'Qamar Bani Hashem' Engineer Brigade augmented by Basiji and the civilian Ministry of Construction often working double shifts. The engineers also prepared a site for the northern end of a pontoon bridge and assembled pre-fabricated bunkers called suleh, to house command teams and troops, while embankments were built to conceal the preparations; yet it does not appear the Iraqis recognised the significance of this activity.[7]

The chronic shortage of military vehicles which forced both the IRIA and Pasdaran to make extensive use of civilian vehicles, including British-built double-decker buses, helped to conceal the movement of troops and supplies. One source suggests that US photographic analysts who examined images of trucks concluded they were being used for commercial traffic, although in 1987 Iraqi Premier, Taha Yassin Ramadan, would claim that the US had 'doctored' their satellite intelligence which meant that the Iraqis were taken by surprise. Farrokh states that, because the Iranians were conscious that US satellites were observing them, they ran streams of trucks, heavy equipment and troops up and down the roads from the Hawizah Marshes to the Basra front to create a heat signature which not only covered the real movements but helped to confuse first the Americans and then Baghdad. In the build-up for the Faw Peninsula attack the most essential transport movements were made at night but there were numerous accidents and a steady stream of injuries, some of them serious.[8]

There was an extensive reconnaissance effort involving naval frogmen, IRIA Special Forces, and the IRIAF which used high performance RF-4E Phantoms and F-5E Tigers, while the Pasdaran

Boats returning to the Iranian side of the Shatt were usually full of casualties. This photograph shows the evacuation of a gruesomely wounded Pasdaran by his comrades, sometime around 11 February 1986. (Tom Cooper Collection)

not only despatched scout units but also used Mohajer Unmanned Aerial Vehicles (UAVs). One encouraging factor was the IRIAF's improvement in combat efficiency after years of decline. Spare parts, acquired either from the black market or from Asian countries, allowed the Iranians to return many aircraft to operational service. By the beginning of Valfajr-8 Iranian sources indicate 140 combat jets were operational, half of them F-5 Tiger IIs. This allowed the IRIAF to assign 12 Tigers and 12 F-14A Tomcats to support the offensive in Operation Shafagh. Interestingly, the IRIAF directives were issued on 5 January by a committee led by Rafsanjari and included a requirement to provide the Pasdaran with close air support for a minimum of 15 days, extendable to a month. HAWK batteries would also be assigned to provide air defence, and during the offensive they would launch 86 missiles which reportedly hit 52 targets.[9]

A unique feature of Valfajr-8 was the use of Pasdaran SEAL-type special forces from the two naval brigades who augmented the

By the time Valfajr-8 was launched, the IRIAF was only capable of providing about 20 close air support sorties. Most of these were flown by F-5E/Fs from the TFB.4 and targeted major Iraqi HQs and supply depots on the Faw Peninsula. (Farzin Nadimi Collection)

The Iranian offensive and Iraqi counterattacks on the Faw set the local fuel depot on fire. The huge, black column of smoke continued rising into the sky for months afterwards, and was a clear orientation mark for both sides. (Tom Cooper Collection)

Naval commandos of the Emir al-Mu'minin Naval Brigade IRGC seen moving along a trench while supporting the Nooh Task Force's advance between Khor Abdullah and the Mamlaha salt beds. (Tom Cooper Collection)

IRIA teams of 23rd Special Forces Division. Four SEAL battalions were deployed with some 2,400 men, although there was a shortage of both wet suits and Scuba gear, but despite this the frogmen began a systematic examination of the southern landing sites from September 1985. Small boats would quietly cross the Shatt and insert the SEALs into the smelly and salty water so they could swim to the Iraqi-held coast. Strong currents made this hard work, indeed they could spend only 2-3 hours in the water, and by the time they were recovered the men were exhausted. Some 700-800 missions were made, usually a simple night reconnaissance, but occasionally the men would conceal themselves in reed beds during the day and sometimes they would go ashore, change into civilian clothing so as to resemble local peasants and tour the enemy rear. More than half the missions were reported to be successful and they provided detailed information on the defences, even to the size of bunker doors!

Iranian preparations and the terrain

Crossing the Shatt (called Arvand by the Iranians) would be a formidable problem and one newly arrived divisional commander was reported to have exclaimed "May God help us; how can we cross the Arvand?" The IRIA bridging inventory was extended during late 1985, including six pontoon bridges from Germany, while some 3,000 small boats were purchased, mostly from Japan, and distributed among the naval brigades' three boat battalions, but with so many non-swimmers thousands of life jackets were also acquired. The Pasdaran learned from their experiences in the Hawizah Marshes in 1984 and 1985 and were able to practice tactics in conditions of tight security on the Caspian.

Hassani-Sa'di decided to give his men the best possible chance of success by launching his assaults when rain would ground enemy air power and low cloud would reduce its effectiveness. He would first launch diversionary operations around the Hawizah Marshes and towards the upper part of the peninsula while airborne troops raided towards Umm Qasr as well as the Mina al-Bakr and Khowr (or Khawr) al-Amayah Al-Amayah offshore oil terminals which lie some 25 nautical miles (45 kilometres) southeast of Faw City.

The Iranians had some two dozen divisions in Khuzestan Province, some 200,000-300,000 men swelled by 50,000 Basiji. Half the divisions were ostentatiously deployed in large tent encampments either on the eastern shores of the Hawizah Marshes or opposite the Fish Lake Line opposite VI and III Corps to divert enemy attention northwards. In addition large numbers of worn-out and leaking boats were also assembled on the marsh edges. Another half-a-dozen divisions were assembled opposite al-Amarah to threaten IV Corps.

The main assault would be launched by the equivalent of nine full-strength divisions who, with support forces, totalled 97,000 men who were secretly assembled south of Khorammshahr, the majority amid the date palms south of Khosrowabad, under the Khatam al-Anbiya Command. They were organised into Task Force Karbala with 7th Vali Asr, 8th Najaf Ashraf, 19th 'Fajr', 27th Mohammad Rasoolallah, 41st 'Sarallah' Divisions, 57th 'Abolfazl al-Abbas' Brigade; 105th 'Al-Kawthar' Naval Brigade (five infantry, one SEAL, one naval battalion) together with the 1st and 2nd Brigades/21st

IRIA Infantry Division, some 48,000 men. Supporting this was Task Force 'Nooh' with some 27,000 men of 14th 'Imam Hossein', 17th Ali Ibn Abu Talib, 25th Karbala Divisions, 104th 'Emir al-Mu'minin' Naval Brigade (Five infantry, three SEAL, two naval battalions). They were supported by the Pasdaran's artillery brigade (believed to be 90th 'Khatam al-Anbiya') and 'Qamar Bani Hashem' Engineer Brigades, and possibly the IRIA 33rd Artillery Group. Although not confirmed by either side, experience in the previous two offensives would have led the Iranians to anticipate chemical attacks. They had quietly acquired chemical protection equipment and it is probable that they had assembled one of the two chemical decontamination brigades to support the operation. There would also be a subsidiary operation by the 1st Brigade/77th IRIA Division with two brigades of 5th "Nassr" Pasdaran Divisions with some 19,000 men.

This subsidiary operation would strike from the mouth of the River Karun to seize the island of Umm al-Rasas (also Omm al-Rasas) as a stepping stone to establishing a beachhead on the peninsula. A pontoon bridge would then be thrown across the Shatt allowing reinforcements to expand the bridgehead while disrupting the movement of enemy reserves down the Basra-al-Faw (Faw City) highway. Iranian sources remain silent upon the ultimate objective of this operation, which may have aimed to provide a springboard for an advance on Basra once the whole of the peninsula was in Iranian hands.

The main blow would be launched across the Shatt from south of Khorammshahr at the southern end of the Faw Peninsula using the two task forces which assembled between Khosrowabad and Arvand Kenar, in the cultivated area around the mouth of the Shatt. Spearheaded by the naval brigades they would cross the Shatt with Karbala on the right and 'Nooh' on the left to seize and secure the southern end of the peninsula. Pontoon bridges would then be thrown across the Shatt allowing the bridgehead to expand north towards Basra and west towards Umm Qasr to establish a significant, brooding, presence along Kuwait's northern border.

The Faw Peninsula lies south of Az Zubayr and Abu al-Khasib (also Abdul Khassib, Abul Khasib, Abu al-Kasib and Abolkhasib), which are some 10-15 kilometres southeast and southwest of Basra respectively and is bounded in the east by the Shatt al Arab and in the west by

An Iranian anti-tank team mounted on a jeep with a 106mm M40 recoilless rifle approaching a burning Iraqi fuel dump in al-Faw. (Tom Cooper Collection)

A Bell AH-1J Cobra underway, passing low over the Shatt al-Arab in the direction of al-Faw. The Iraqis amassed an immense volume of anti-aircraft defences on their side of the frontline, attempting to close the skies for Iranian fliers. Therefore, their appearance was always a morale-bolster for Iranian ground troops. (Tom Cooper Collection)

Further Iranian advances north of Faw resulted in the capture of this Thomson-CSF Rasit battlefield surveillance radar and a Chinese-made Type-69 MBT. (Farzin Nadimi Collection)

Also captured by Iranians at Faw was the full complement of an Iraqi SA-6 SAM-site. Although operated by the Iraqi Army, these weapons systems were usually reserved for the defence of major communication and supply-centres in the rear of Iraqi the lines. (Farzin Nadimi Collection)

the Khowr Abdullah. It is some 90 kilometres long, ending at the Ras al-Bisha (al-Bisha Cape), and a maximum of 50 kilometres wide and, apart from a 6 kilometre wide strip of firm ground along the east, it consists largely of brackish salt marshes (Hawr ah-Ahwar) which dry out in the summer, except in the west where a strip up to 15 kilometres wide remains permanently flooded. The most densely populated part of the peninsula is an agricultural area 2-4 kilometres wide down the Shatt coast, where fields and dense date-palm groves, surrounded by low mud walls, are watered by numerous irrigation channels. A score of little villages are to be found in this area together with the region's largest town, Faw City, which had some 70,000 inhabitants at the outbreak of the war (although almost all had subsequently fled north). On the northern and eastern outskirts of the town, separated by the Basra-Faw City highway, were oil tanks which had fed the two terminals but were now scorched and twisted metal.

There were numerous paths and small gravel-topped or beaten earth roads on embankments across the peninsula, including one running beside the Shatt, but there were only two major roads which ran northwest to southeast from Abu al-Khasib, one being a 'hard-top' (asphalt) coastal highway from Basra to Faw City which is just inland from the cultivated belt. The other ran down the middle of the peninsula to join the Basra road just north of Faw City and until 1985 had been gravel-topped then given an asphalt covering. Some 10 kilometres from Faw City this road ran down the northeastern side of the Mamlaha (sometimes written Memlaha) salt beds with an evaporator complex consisting of nine salt-extraction ponds in an 8 kilometre x 8 kilometre area divided by a 1.2-metre high earth bund. The southwestern edge of these salt beds was a canal to drain the Hawr ah-Ahwar marshes and this then ran 12 kilometres eastwards to the oil tanks south of the Basra-Faw City highway before taking a 6 kilometre detour to the south then returning almost to the highway.

Another asphalt-topped road ran westwards from Faw City along the peninsula's southern coast, where low tide created wide mud flats, to pass the other side of the ponds before reaching Umm Qasr which lies on the other side of the Khowr Abdullah. The town, which had some 50,000 inhabitants, is separated from

This Iraqi ZSU-23-4 became bogged down in the mud and was then abandoned by its owners. The Iranians captured the vehicle and one of their troops can be seen conducting repairs on it, but in the light of fierce of Iraqi counterattacks, it is unlikely that this Shilka survived for very much longer. (Farzin Nadimi Collection)

A stretcher party of IRGC Naval commandos seen crossing the pontoon bridge over the Shatt al-Arab while carrying a wounded comrade to the field hospital. (Tom Cooper Collection)

Kuwait by a small inlet and was created in 1958 as a naval base which was expanded three years later into the country's only deep water port. It was completed in July 1967 and linked to Basra by both a highway and a railway running along the western banks of the Khowr Abdullah through Zubayr.

Intelligence games

The Iraqis were aware of the build-up north of Khorammshah and Abadan, assisted, probably indirectly, by US satellite intelligence which detected the Iranian build-up north of Basra, but the rainy-season clouds had obscured the ground south of the city. Consequently Baghdad was most concerned by the assembly of some six divisions (50,000 men) in the Susangerd area and concluded the main blow would land around al-Amarah, north of the Hawizah Marshes, in IV Corps or, between there and Qurnah, as with Khyber and Badr, against VI Corps. The Iranians had indeed planned to strike towards Qurnah but only as a diversion, possibly because Rashid's Army Day offensive made a stronger blow impossible by depriving the southern-most prong of a springboard.

But the main blow was always scheduled to fall some 40 kilometres to the south and the Iraqi failure to detect enemy preparations for this blow, despite their superiority in COMINT, was due to a number of factors. Primarily, COMINT proved of little help because the Pasdarans' lack of radios forced them to rely upon landlines or motorcycle couriers, although their reliance upon IRIA logistical support which was better equipped with radios, did pose a security threat. GMID was also being fed false information by double or turned agents including a spy caught in Ahwaz. Pasdaran leader Rahim Safavi noted that the latter 'was under our control and communicated the information that we wanted.[10]

Iraqi COMINT did detect at least one message which suggested plans for an offensive against the Faw Peninsula but it was not passed on, yet the Iraqi Navy clearly received concrete information about enemy intentions for it withdrew its 'Silkworm' coast defence missiles from a base just south of Faw City. Several senior Iraqi generals visited the Faw Peninsula and reported they could see boats being assembled, extensive road building, and gaps in the palm groves for supply dumps, but the head of the GMID since August 1983, Major General Mahmood Shukur Shahin discounted

While officially exported to Iraq as 'VIP-transports', and supposedly equipped for such purposes only, German-made Bo.105 helicopters were actually attack helicopters, usually armed with 20mm cannons and launchers for unguided rockets. They were deployed in large numbers during the fighting at Faw. (Ali Tobchi Collection)

Iranian troops inside the captured Iraqi air defence centre outside al-Faw. The HQ in question was responsible for the air defence of much of southern Iraq, and its loss was badly felt by the IrAF. (Farzin Nadimi Collection)

The Iraqi Air Force hit back at Iranian troops with all available aircraft, from fighter-bombers like this pair of MiG-23BNs – seen deploying FAB-100 bombs – to medium bombers like Tupolev Tu-16s and Tu-22s. (Tom Cooper Collection)

An M192 triple launcher for the MIM-23B I-HAWK SAM. The Iranians developed an elaborate air defence system for Operation Valfajr-8, in which HAWK SAMs played a major role. (Farzin Nadimi Collection)

them claiming it was an obvious deception.[11] However, he was not the only one to be mistaken about Iranian intentions. Washington analysed the Iranian concentrations and alerted Saddam through his friend King Hussein of Jordan that the attack upon Faw would be only 'a limited assault'. The main blow, the king said, 'would come later in the central sector.' Knowing the origin of this information, which confirmed reports from their own intelligence organisation, it was little wonder the Iraqis were totally surprised.

Defending the peninsula

Until April or May 1984 the peninsula was part of III Corps' TAOR, but the 'Ramadan' and Khyber offensives demonstrated the Basra-based corps needed to focus on threats from the north and the east. The Faw Peninsula was regarded as being a minor front facing commando raids, starting on 10 May 1982 during Operations Beit-ol-Moqaddas when Iranian naval commandoes struck the peninsula's Ras al-Bisha radar station which was used to monitor shipping movements. At the time of the Khyber offensive it was garrisoned by three border guard brigades, 238th Infantry Brigade, and the Navy, with a brigade of 6th Armoured Division and 33rd Special Forces Brigade available as a reaction force. Khyber demonstrated the Pasdaran could pose a serious threat to such a ragbag of units and in May 1985 the peninsula was placed under the new Shatt al Arab Operations Headquarters (SAOH) or Quiadet Amaliyat Shatt al-Arab (Shatt al-Arab Operations Command) in Arabic. This covered the western bank of the Shatt al Arab and the southern coast of the Faw Peninsula to Umm Qasr, but in March or August 1985 this was upgraded to VII Corps.[12]

The corps' first commander was Major General Shawkat Ahmed Atta, the former Director of Military Operations who had drafted the documents which created the EOTH in 1984.[13] By early 1986 this had some 27,000 men under Major General Shawkat Ahmed Atta who had eight brigades with a nominal 15,000 men evenly split between the 15th ('Farooq Force') Infantry Division and 26th Infantry Division. The latter exercised the operational control of the 441st Naval Brigade in the south, but not the 440th Naval Brigade at Umm Qasr.[14]

Both formations were stretched to the limit along the 170-kilometre Shatt front, and even if they had been at full strength they would have had about 100 men per kilometre in a situation ominously similar to the one the Iraqis faced along the Karun at the start of the Iranian Operation Beit-ol-Moqaddas in 1982. The 26th Division was especially vulnerable with its northernmost brigade holding a 21 kilometre front while the others each had lines of 40-50 kilometres. Baghdad was confident there was no major threat to the peninsula, especially in the south, and drained

Wreckage of an Iraqi Su-22M-3 (serial 4078) shot down by the Iranians during the Valfajr-8 Offensive. While the Iranians claimed over 70 Iraqi aircraft and helicopters as shot down, the Iraqis admitted only about 16 losses. (Farzin Nadimi Collection)

The IrAF paid a hefty price while attempting to counterattack Iranian ground forces on the Faw Peninsula. This dramatic photograph shows a burning Iraqi Su-22M-3 going down over the Shatt al-Arab, opposite Abadan in Iran. (Farzin Nadimi Collection)

IRIAF personnel seen while re-loading a MIM-23B I-HAWK missiles on its launcher. This missile could reach speeds of up to Mach 2.5. Additional rounds for this system were acquired within the frame of the so-called 'Irangate Affair', later in 1986. (Farzin Nadimi Collection)

Ata's command of men and equipment to IV Corps especially, where Shawkat was attached until the eve of the Iranian attack as an assistant and potential replacement. While the divisions had commando battalions, and the brigades had commando companies as reaction forces, Ata lacked a formal 'fire brigade' in the shape of a commando force apart from an ad hoc reserve group of about 1,000 men, possibly drawn from 66th Commando Brigade south of Basra, while his total fire support consisted of only four field artillery battalions (72 guns) and three heavy mortar batteries. During the lull in the fighting in the late summer of 1985 Shawkat persuaded Baghdad to provide him with engineers and heavy equipment. He used them to improve the road network, especially around the cultivated area, and to build a berm, together with bunkers and vehicle shelters, along the eastern side of the Basra-Faw City highway, which would prove a valuable asset during the crisis. He had also improved the road down the centre of the peninsula and built a few switch positions to restrict commando penetrations, but the combination of Defence Ministry indifference and terrain prevented the construction of a defensive system in depth.[15]

During Valfajr-8, the IRGC pressed even such old weapons as this US-built 40mm M1 L/60 anti-aircraft gun into service. This weapon could fire 120 rounds per minute and target aircraft out to a range of 7,000 metres. It proved deadly not only against low-flying helicopters, but also against infantry exposed in the open. (Tom Cooper Collection)

Early warning was the first line of defence based upon a string of Rasit battlefield surveillance radars whose antennas were either on masts or the tops of bunkers, but they were designed for use over land rather than water which degraded their performance. These were augmented by searchlights and watch towers for visual observation using night vision goggles. Between the water and the shore were two lines, six metres deep, of wire-covered steel-beam obstacles similar to the 'Czech hedgehogs' deployed on the Normandy beaches by the Germans in 1944. Close to the shore was a line of pre-fabricated bunkers, usually consisting of a buried steel frame covered with corrugated steel sheets, then concrete or earth and then 50 centimetres of gravel, up to a metre thick. These were sited for all-round defence with wire obstacles and 800-1,000 metres behind them would be command bunkers and artillery battery positions.[16]

One of the Iraqi aircraft lost to reinforced Iranian air defences was this Mi-25 helicopter gunship (serial number either 2110 or 2121). The helicopter was disabled by ground fire, but the crew managed to land safely. The Mi-25 was subsequently brought to Tehran, where it is still on display. (Farzin Nadimi Collection)

The tip of the peninsula was the responsibility of 700 sailors and 500 airmen, mostly technical troops with little or no combat training. The former formed part of 2nd Naval Brigade, with three launchers on earth mounds for Chinese-made CSS-2 'Silkworm' anti-ship missiles, supported by a Garpun ('Plank Shave') surface search radar, or the Chinese Type-352 ('Square Tie'), and a command post. The airmen were from the Southern Air Defence Command, which had a site just north of al-Faw City, possibly linked into the Kuwaiti and other Gulf State air defence systems. It was equipped with French Tigre (Tiger), and possibly the Soviet 'Long Track', air search radars and there were also four surface-to-air missile sites with Crotale and SA-6 'Gainful' missiles, the former supported by Mirador II and 'Straight Flush' search and target acquisition radars.[17]

Holding the southern coast of the peninsula and shielding Umm Qasr was the 1,000-man, relatively lightly armed 441st Naval Brigade raised from Rear Admiral Abd Muhammad Abdullah's under-employed navy of some 3,000 men, and more of a coast defence militia and guard force than a full brigade, indeed it also supplied men for defending the Hawizah Marshes. The Navy itself

Although the sky over the Faw Peninsula was heavily infested by all sorts of air defences, Iraqi pilots continued flying fierce counterattacks with all available aircraft and helicopters. Here a Gazelle is taking off from one of the forward heliports close to the frontlines, armed with launchers for unguided rockets. (Ali Tobchi Collection)

Table 8: IRGC, Khatam al-Anbiya Command, February 1986

Corps	Division & HQ	Brigades & Notes
	Direct Combat Support Group (IRIAA)	2 attack battalions (AH-1Js), 2 assault battalions (Bell 214As), 1 reconnaissance battalion (Bell 206), 1 transport battalion (CH-47C)
	33rd Artillery Group	3 battalions of M109; 1 battery of M107; 3 battalions of towed artillery pieces; 1 MRLS-battalion (total of about 90 artillery pieces and 12 BM-21s)
Task Force Karbala	21st Infantry Division (IRIA)	1st Brigade only
	7th Vali Asr Infantry Division (IRGC)	
	8th Najaf Ashraf Infantry Division (IRGC)	
	19th Fajr Infantry Division (IRGC)	
	27th Mohammad Rasoolallah Infantry Division (IRGC)	
	41st Sarallah Infantry Division (IRGC)	
		57th Abolfazl al-Abbas Infantry Brigade (IRGC)
		105th al-Kawthar Naval Infantry Brigade (IRGC; including 5 naval infantry, and 2 commando battalions)
Task Force Nooh	14th Imam Hossein Infantry Division (IRGC)	
	17th Ali Ibn Abu Talib Infantry Division (IRGC)	
	25th Karbala Infantry Division (IRGC)	
		90th Khatam al-Anbiya Artillery Brigade
		Qamar Bani Hashem Engineer brigade (IRGC)
Task Force Nasr	5th Nasr Infantry Division (IRGC)	
	77th Infantry Division (IRIA)	1st Brigade only; reinforced by 2 brigades from the 5th Nassr Infantry Division (IRGC)
		104th Emir al-Mu'mim Naval Infantry Brigade (IRGC; including 5 infantry, 3 commando and 2 artillery battalions)
Reserve and Diversionary Forces	81st Armoured Division (IRIA)	1 brigade only
	92nd Armoured Division (IRIA)	2nd Armoured Brigade only
		55th Airborne Brigade (IRIA)

Table 9: III and VII Corps Iraqi Army, February 1986

Corps	Division	Brigades & Notes
III Corps	Corps Troops	8th Border Brigade; 33rd SF Brigade; 65th Commando Brigade; III Corps Artillery Brigade (10 artillery and 5 MRLS-batteries)
	11th Infantry Division	45th and 47th Infantry Brigades
	19th Infantry Division	
	30th Infantry Division	
	31st Infantry Division	49th and 109th Infantry Brigades
VII Corps	Corps Troops	66th Commando Brigade (elements), 440th Naval Infantry Brigade; VII Corps Artillery Brigade (4 field artillery battalions, 72 tubes)
	15th Infantry Division	44th, 104th, 501st and 802nd Infantry Brigades
	26th Infantry Division	110th, 111th, and 440th Infantry Brigades
Navy		2nd Naval Brigade (CSS-2 AShM)
		441st Naval Infantry Brigade (subordinated to 26th Infantry Division)
Reserve Forces & Reinforcements	Republican Guards Armoured Division	3rd Republican Guards SF Brigade; 4th Republican Guards Infantry Brigade
	5th Mechanised Division	15th and 20th Mechanised Brigades
	6th Armoured Division	16th, 30th and 56th Armoured Brigades; 25th Mechanised Brigade
	14th Infantry Division	
		224th Missile Brigade (2 SCUD battalions, 10 TELs)

had some 30 vessels, none of which had a gun greater than 37mm calibre – which meant they were largely unsuitable for taking part in ground combat.

Crossing the Shatt

For the Iranians everything now depended upon the weather and the need for low cloud, rain and fog to shield their forces, with the window of opportunity likely to open from late January and, in this case, the rain began to fall during the last three days of the month. Under low, dark, clouds the final preparations began, with the decision to launch the offensive probably made on 8 February, which gave Rafsanjari and Rezai time to travel to the command post, the latter carrying a green banner from the shrine of Imam Reza which he presented to the Karbala commander. The troops moved out during the night from 9 to 10 February after first praying, then having their supper. Their prayers were answered, for from 1800 hrs it began to drizzle, and as the men assembled an hour later the rain grew heavier.[18]

SEALs spearheaded the offensive, but the continued shortage of wet suits weakened their operations. Yet undeterred, they set off in small boats through choppy waters, which capsized one or two boats causing the frogmen to lose their weapons including assault rifles and RPGs. As they sailed, the weather briefly improved, and the men entered the water at about 2000 hrs under moonlight obscured by patches of cloud, though within a couple of hours it would turn stormy again with high winds and heavy rain.

Off the Iraqi coast the SEALs lowered themselves into the water, taking up to an hour to swim to the shore, but all had pledged not to return without completing their missions. Many rested in the reeds under radio silence while preparing to penetrate the obstacle belt and enter the bunkers, while others placed demolition charges on obstacles to clear a path for the first infantry wave. The SEALs began isolating the bunkers where many of the defenders were sheltering from the heavy rain or were sleeping. Simultaneously, demolition teams detonated charges on the obstacles, which was the signal for the boats carrying the infantry wave, waiting offshore in overloaded boats, to begin their assault. Yet it was only at 2210 hrs that the Iranian headquarters broadcast the go-code 'Oh Fatemeh al-Zahra' to the divisions which then passed it on down the chain of command.[19]

Iranian artillery battalions, with Pasdaran fire support units, now bombarded the bunkers, which faced a rain of shells from guns and recoilless artillery, rockets and mortar bombs, although some of the Pasdaran fire was a waste of ammunition. The bombardment and the sounds of approaching boats were the defenders' first warning that they were under threat, and some fled as the leading wave of Pasdaran infantry arrived having endured a waterborne ordeal which would have had many saying their prayers with greater fervour. They happily leaped waist-deep into the water to begin assaulting the bunkers opposite the six chosen beachheads. Some bunkers were engaged from boats offshore and within 30 minutes the first was captured. The infantry then began to push inland, joined by SEALs who stripped off their wet suits into regular

Crew of an Iraqi T-62 tank platoon receiving a briefing on their next mission. Tanks spearheaded every Iraqi counterattack on the Faw Peninsula, but the terrain restricted their operations to the immediate vicinity of roads. (Tom Cooper Collection)

In the words of several interviewed Iraqi officers, the Faw Campaign was 'eating' men and machines at amazing pace. This Iraqi Type-69 was photographed while rolling in the direction of the battlefield in March 1986. (Tom Cooper Collection)

uniforms, while artillery observers, sometimes using captured watch towers, directed fire inland.

North of the Shatt, the 'Oh Fatemeh al-Zahra' go-code triggered a series of diversionary operations which exploded along the front like firecrackers, from the Hawizah Marshes towards Qurnah, and others against the Fish Lake Line, while Basra was also shelled. The attack on the defences north of the Fish Lake were spearheaded by 2nd Brigade of the 92nd Armoured Division – supported by the Pasdaran of the 12th Qa'em-e Mohamad Mechanised Division: this was certainly a significant commitment of Iran's much-depleted armoured forces. They struck the 19th (Major General Talal Muhammad Salih) and 30th (Brigadier Naijim ad-Din Abdullah) Infantry Divisions of Major General Rashid's III Corps over drier, firmer ground to the south.

Salih's division had been forewarned and, remembering the lessons of its Khyber debut in February 1984, had turned no-man's-land into an artillery-covered killing ground of wire entanglements and minefields, and so the enemy did not come within 150 metres of their positions. Abdullah's division, presumably also alerted, beat off three attacks on the first night almost without breaking sweat, and was not significantly troubled afterwards.

Four days later, from dawn on 14 February, there was an attempt to push the 31st Infantry Division (Brigadier Yalshin Umar Abdil) off South Majnoon with Pasdaran, later supported by 2nd Brigade/92nd IRIA Armoured Division. The Iranians copied the enemy's Army Day tactics, using boats to land all over the island and with heavy artillery support from North Majnoon, and they again pushed 49th and 109th Infantry Brigades into a small bridgehead despite vigorous counter-attacks.

The main thrust was along the Basra-Khorramshahr highway against 11th Infantry Division (Brigadier Abd al-Zahra Shkara al-Maliki) against (north to south) 47th and 45th Infantry Brigades by brigades of 81st Armoured, 21st and 77th IRIA Infantry Divisions. The Iranians managed to fight their way through heavy artillery fire to take a nearby island, and along the river bank then gained a foothold in 47th Infantry Brigade's position, inflicting heavy losses. During the afternoon of 11 February a 5th Mechanised Division counter-attack recovered the lost positions and drove back the enemy who then tried to outflank 45th Brigade with an amphibious attack but were beaten off. The attacks upon III Corps were largely repulsed from strong defences using well-rehearsed tactics based upon massive artillery, as well as air, support with the IrAF and IrAAC flying some 984 sorties from 10-12 February, yet it helped to confuse the Iraqi Army command. They probably cost III Corps some 4,000 casualties and the attackers about 8,000.

The Iranians added to the confusion by flying elements of 55th Airborne Brigade from a small air base on Jazireh-ye Dara (Dara Island), some 35 kilometres south of Bandar-e Khomeini in raids against oil terminals and even Umm Qasr itself. The attempt to establish a landing site near the latter was thwarted by vigilant sentries, while fire from the equally alert oil platform garrisons also prevented landings. Yet as reports of heliborne attacks flooded into the peninsula the defenders began to fire wildly and fruitlessly into the skies.

On the Faw Peninsula the bid to establish the northern bridgehead was made by 77th Division and Nassr, which landed on the Iraqi divisional boundary, striking 15th Infantry Division's southern flank unit, the 104th Infantry Brigade. The first landing was on Umm al-Rasas, 'a waterlogged sandbar between Basra and Faw...' which consisted of '... some date palm plantations and the remains of some tiny villages which had once been connected to the mainland by a metal-type pontoon bridge'.[20] With the island secure the Iranians tried to seize this bridge to access the peninsula while beginning the construction of four of their own pontoon bridges across the Shatt. The 104th Brigade fell back into a switch line: the Iranians took 14 hours to overcome it again, by when the 15th Division had assembled reinforcements that finally contained their – meanwhile about two kilometres deep – bridgehead.

Chaos

Throughout the peninsula some defenders showed resolution which slowed the advance but, as Iranian COMINT confirmed, in many places the Iraqi defences dissolved into confusion and panic. Corps commander Shawkat was slow to respond, partly because many brigade and battalion commanders not only failed to report counter-attacks accurately or to promptly, but also tried to down-play the scale of the threat – out of a mixture of ignorance and habit. Consequently, Shawkat – who had previously boasted that he would drive any invader into the sea – was slow to recognise the scale of the emerging disaster. However, with daylight the defenders did slowly gain in strength as they determined the enemy's crossing sites and gunners began to range on them with both high-explosive and shells filled with chemical agents. These greatly hampered the forward movement of Iranian men and supplies. The decision to use chemical weapons was made on 11 February with their delivery made by 56 aircraft and three battalions of 155m guns which could call upon a stock of 2,000 bombs and 10,000 shells, respectively, delivering 100 of the former and up to 250 of the latter per day.[21] Air attacks were a threat until HAWK batteries came on-stream and claimed 20 aircraft on 11 February forcing the IrAF to operate in strike packages each supported Mirage F.1EQ fighter-bombers equipped with French-made Caiman stand-off jamming pods. Hovercraft and helicopters augmented the boats to move Pasdaran troops, anti-armour teams and artillery across the water as guns on the eastern bank pounded Iraqi defences.

The failure to complete and deploy the pontoon bridges meant the Iranians could not bring over armour or artillery and while many Pasdaran had been taught to drive Iraqi armour, and the Iranians claimed to have captured 120 AFVs by 12 February, the attackers captured few drivable vehicles and those which did fall into their hands were deployed late and often piecemeal in close and marshy terrain where many were destroyed. By now Rashid's III Corps had transferred 6th Armoured Division to support Ata who committed it on the 15 Division front on 12 February together with 3rd Guards Special Forces and 4th Guards Infantry Brigades which had been flown south from Baghdad and rushed by trucks driving at top speed through torrential rain to the new front.

They were hastily assembled to spearhead a co-ordinated counter-attack on the morning of 12 February, but as the companies formed up they were subjected to a fierce rocket bombardment from batteries of Iranian BM-21 Grad MRLS on the other side of the Shatt which delayed their attack and caused up to 30% losses.[22] Air strikes with chemical weapons were called in but with the combatants so close some hit friendly troops. They recovered quickly and pushed forward with strong air support, but tanks were frequently bogged down and the haste with which the counter-attack was arranged was reflected in poor coordination. Although Pasdaran positions were penetrated some forward units were exposed, which led to close quarter fighting before the Guards, having suffered severe casualties and the loss of much equipment, were eventually rescued by army units, but their sacrifice ended all hopes of a further Pasdaran advance.[23]

Ata had also received 66th Commando Brigade (Brigadier Bariq Abdallah) which was landed by assault boats on Umm al-Rasas on the evening of 11 February. Supported by 15th Division's artillery and the new Brazilian Astros MRLS, it retook the island after 18 hours of bitter, close quarter fighting. With the loss of their prime bridging point and already suffering from gas attacks, the Iranians re-crossed the Shatt.

Potentially the most serious threat came on the southern end of the peninsula as the two task forces exploited the SEAL success, landing half-an-hour after the northern bridgehead and reaching the Basra-Faw City highway by 0300 hrs which was exploited to expand the bridgehead as the defence collapsed in confusion. Iranian COMINT reportedly intercepted an exchange, apparently between 26th Division and 111th Brigade, which reported the destruction of 110th Brigade and one of its own battalions, and the isolation of half another. The exchange concluded with the two officers exchanging insults as Iraqi troops were captured when their vehicles stopped to ask the advancing Iranians what was happening. But the Iranians found it difficult to exploit the situation due to the shortages of vehicles and limited radio communications – divisions had only 2-5 radio operators while in trying to direct operations from the north bank many commanders became hoarse.[24]

Task Force Karbala, led by 1st Brigade/21st Division, and 'Fajr' in the north started well by pushing 26th Division's 111th Brigade northward in a fighting retreat up the peninsula although its commander was captured on 12 February. Vali Asr' made a separate landing and linked up with 'Fajr' in the palm groves. Despite its command post being overrun and severe losses, the brigade delayed the Iranians long enough for 6th Armoured Division to send down 16th Armoured Brigade with some commandoes to stabilise the situation. A major obstacle to the advance was a large bunker on the highway, which they called Konj (Corner), at a point where it met a minor road some 15 kilometres northwest of Faw City and 5 kilometres south of Kut Nughaymish. It required two brigades to take it and the effort apparently exhausted the attackers who established a berm-based defensive line, some four kilometres long, where they went onto the defensive as growing Iraqi forces came down the coastal highway.

The Meatgrinder

On 11 February the Iraqis began to push southwards along the coastal highway towards the Konj, but mud and mines hastily laid on the roadside verges confined this attack to the road which was blocked with a berm manned by Pasdarans with Basiji in front. The attackers were stopped and driven back in confusion under attack from Cobra gunships which bought time for Iranian engineers to dig an anti-armour ditch. Meanwhile, the Najaf Ashraf Division then began to advance westwards from the highway towards the Mamlaha salt pans, skilfully using TOW and 'Sagger' missiles, as well as towed MRLS, to overcome resistance from road embankments or berms.

Iraqi attacks grew in strength and from 12 February the Republican Guards tried to push south towards the Konj, although progress was disrupted by an accidental IrAF chemical strike. The Guards' T-72 tanks were largely impervious to Iranian anti-armour missiles but were still confined to the road and the immediate surroundings, while due to the Najaf Ashraf advance westwards the Iranians were in an exposed salient, and to shore up the defences the Mohammad Rasoolallah Division and 'Abolfazl al-Abbas' Brigade were brought up; the latter to support Najaf Ashrafs continued advance westwards during the night. In many cases the Pasdaran crawled for up to a kilometre, their progress lit by flares from Iraqi PC-7s, they then

An unusual weapon deployed by the Iranians for the first time during Operation Valfajr-8 were Mohajeer UAVs. Originally based on the design of Israeli UAVs shoot down over Lebanon, Mohajeers were primarily designed and deployed for reconnaissance. However, Iranians armed several examples with RPG-7s, thus deploying the first ever 'unmanned combat aerial vehicle' (UCAV) in combat. (Farzin Nadimi Collection)

The crew of an Iranian ZPU-1 machine gun (single-barrel version of the 14.5mm KPV machinegun), preparing their weapon for action at Faw. (Albert Grandolini Collection)

surprised the few defenders to fight their way into the salt pans.

But by pushing so far forward, Task Force Karbala exposed the

Iranian northern front and on the afternoon of 13 February an Iraqi attack inflicted heavy losses upon the Mohammad Rasoolallah Division and opened the right of the 'Abolfazl al-Abbas' Brigade until the arrival of the 'Imam Hossein' Brigade aided by 23mm anti-aircraft guns which hosed down the attacking infantry. The growing pressure slowly forced the Iranians back towards the Konj, the Pasdaran desperately buying time while engineers of the Construction Ministry hastily threw up a defensive berm which was completed that night, shielded by fierce counter-attacks against a newly arrived Iraqi commando brigade. The new defences helped to stabilise the Iranian line whose defenders beat off attacks over the next three days to 15 February, and this would mark the high point of the Iranian advance.

To the south, Task Force 'Nooh' reached the coastal highway at about 0300 hours and, spearheaded by the Karbala Division, moved rapidly towards Faw City rolling up the southern brigades of Brigadier General Mirza Hamza as-Sultani's 26th Division. Karbala was briefly delayed by a half-hearted counter-attack which it beat off, and after this token resistance many of the defending officers and men (including Mirza Sultani) reportedly fled in panic abandoning, according to the Iranians, 30 MBTs and Cascaval APCs. Karbala isolated Faw City before dawn, but then the divisional commander defied orders to lead a brigade into the salt pans only to be stopped by 441st Brigade fighting from berms 3-4 kilometres west of the city, although they were unable to prevent the Iranians overrunning the 110th Brigade's command post and a surface-to-air missile base. Meanwhile, the Mohammad Rasoolallah Division on Task Force Karbala's left further isolated Faw City by cutting the secondary road to Zubayr. Joined by the Ali Ibn Abu Talib Division, the Karbala Division assaulted the town during the morning, in heavy rain, to occupy both it and 26th Division headquarters, capturing 950 prisoners and some 40 anti-aircraft guns.

Karbala continued to the al-Bisha Cape which fell just after midnight of 11 February, despite desperate resistance by the Iraqi sailors and marines, but with the 'Silkworm' missiles having been withdrawn to Umm Qasr all the Iranians captured were two launchers and 100 prisoners. Many of the latter had tried to wade the mud flats and been trapped to their waists until pulled out by the Pasdaran after they found their abandoned boots on the shore line. There are reports that some Iraqi senior officers escaped in hovercraft with key components from the missile and radar systems as well as electronic warfare equipment. Yet the loss of a key Iraqi air defence facility, which the Iranians blew up a few days later, caused temporary panic in the Gulf Arab capitals. Now lacking coastal surveillance radars, the IrAF found it more difficult to interdict enemy maritime traffic in the northern part of the Gulf.[25]

Having consolidated its positions, Task Force 'Nooh' began to push westwards along the Umm Qasr road during the evening of 11 February with its right covered by the Mohammad Rasoolallah Division. Within half-an-hour it ran into determined Iraqi resistance from 441st Naval Brigade, joined by 440th Naval Brigade, which used the Mamlaha salt works as a strongpoint to prevent the enemy advancing up the Umm Qasr road, the reinforced concrete buildings reducing casualties from air bursts.[26] There was fierce hand-to-hand combat, punctuated by MRLS bombardment, and while the Pasdaran succeeded in taking the salt pans Iraqi reinforcements slowed their advance across the open ground to the north and soon the Iranians were building defensive berms. The Iranian advance was further slowed by the muddy conditions in which both sides fought in slime up to their knees and this accumulated on boots and clothing to such a degree it sometimes made it heavier than the equipment they were carrying in their webbing and haversacks. However, the marshy terrain absorbed the worst effects of Iraqi shells and chemical weapons while Iraqi armour was restricted to the roads and was vulnerable to Cobra helicopter gunships with TOW missiles, as well as anti-armour teams.

A feature of the Iranian operations was the air support it received from both the IRIAF and the IRIAA. They interdicted armour on the roads south from Basra, while transport helicopters deployed Pasdaran 'Zolfagha' anti-armour teams with RPG-7s. This forced the Iraqis to organise Helicopter Combat Patrols, some using the propeller-driven PC-7s often with Border Guard or instructor pilots. Problems bringing forward their artillery forced the Iranians to use air power as compensation, but from 9-18 February Iranian records show an average of 40 CAS sorties a day out of a daily total of 100 combat air sorties. This number dropped to 18 a day until the end of February and then a dozen.[27]

The IrAF interdiction of communications started on 11 February when pairs of aircraft began appearing at five-minute intervals, although they tended to attack from too high and were rarely accurate. Between 9 and 13 February, when rain grounded both sides' airmen for a day, the Iraqis flew 1,198 fixed-wing and 596 rotary-wing sorties, and between 15 and 23 February, despite frequent rain showers and fog, 3,046 fixed-wing and 2,235 rotary-wing sorties. The interdiction campaign was also hampered by air defences and the IrAF had a very limited night attack capability. The Iraqis also struck communications along the Iranian side of the Shatt al Arab but most of the damage was quickly repaired and the Iraqis were unable to cut the numerous bridges across the canals and channels. The pontoon bridges were also damaged and had to be floated under cover during the daylight hours until the radar of an I-HAWK battery on Abadan Island was repaired on the afternoon of 11 February. It then launched a dozen missiles to claim 10 victories.

Exhaustion sets in

While the fighting raged on, by 12 February 'Wal Fajr 8' was running out of steam due to shortages of supplies and heavy weapons. On the first night there was chaos on the northern bank because the Iranians underestimated the number of men they needed to move supplies to the boats, forcing commanders to draft command post personnel, including clerics and even follow-up infantry, to carry supplies down the slippery river bank, and then waist deep through icy water. After three or four hours these men were exhausted.

One of the pontoon bridges had been completed on the night of 7 to 8 February and was assembled underwater with attached containers of compressed air which would raise it to the surface. A combination of rough water, the current, and the need to prepare both banks of the Shatt meant it was not deployed until the night of 10 to 11 February after intense engineering work, and was soon augmented by three others. Some 20,000 troops, many of them engineers with earth-moving equipment, crossed on the first night and IRIA engineers brought stocks of anti-armour and anti-personnel mines which the Pasdaran began to plant on the verges of the main roads while their comrades began to build metre-high embankments and strongpoints to consolidate their hold.[28]

Even with the pontoon bridges Iranian logistics faced a major threat from the IrAF which ensured that from 0700 hrs daylight movement across the Shatt largely ceased until nightfall. IrAF attacks forced the Iranians to partly dismantle the bridges at dawn and bring them under cover of land-based air defences. Boats and hovercraft could operate at all times but had to stop each day when the tide ebbed leaving mudflats which could not bear the weight of vehicles, artillery or even individual soldiers. Unloading was disrupted by poison gas, mostly mustard but with some Tabun nerve agents, hanging around the beach-heads to cause some casualties, although the need to wear respirators while undergoing heavy manual labour was probably the greatest problem.[29]

This combination of factors meant that the supply of much engineering equipment, heavy weapons and armour, including MBTs was, according to the Iranians, too little and too late. The Pasdaran also faced the problem of distributing their supplies because the boggy conditions stopped their pick-up trucks. Instead forward units had to rely upon small quantities brought up by motorcycle, or upon captured weapons and ammunition, although the situation eased when the first pontoon bridge to the al-Bisha Cape was completed on the morning of 13 February, and in the early afternoon BMPs brought ammunition up to the front line, now 20 kilometres long, shielding a 50-square-kilometre bridgehead. Later the second bridge was established between Abu Direh, in Iran, and Maamir, 5 kilometres north of Faw City, on the peninsula.

Shortly after the initial crisis had passed, Saddam recalled Shawkat to Baghdad about 17 February to face the General Command's investigation committee, but he was not held responsible. In part this was a recognition that his superiors had stripped him of resources, but the fact he had also been a high-school friend of Saddam probably did not effect his defence. He was initially appointed General Secretary of the Armed Forces General Command, but by 1987 the British Defence Attaché reported he was commanding II Corps. He was replaced by former III Corps commander Major General Sa'di Tu'mah al-Jaburi while General Mirza Sultani, the 26th Division's mediocre commander, was relieved (after the war would rise to the rank of lieutenant general and would die shortly after the 2003 invasion of Iraq). He was replaced by the equally mediocre Brigadier General Amjed Mohammed Hassan who would himself be relieved once the situation on the Faw Peninsula had calmed down.[30]

International Concern
The Iranian presence on the north bank of the Khowr Abdullah, only a few kilometres away deeply worried the Kuwaitis. Iranian President Khamenei now warned them not to allow the Iraqis to use nearby Bubiyan Island (Jazirat Bubiyan) – which controled the waterway – and threatened to confiscate the oil in the Neutral Zone between Kuwait and Saudi Arabia, which was being used to supply Iraqi's customers. On 15 February the Emir of Kuwait, Jaber al-Ahmad al-Jaber as-Sabah, visited the island and publicly declared it to be neutral territory. The Iranian threat increased Saudi fears however, and King Fahd reportedly telephoned Saddam Hussein on 12 February, which led to four high-level meetings in Riyadh and Baghdad during the following fortnight.

In late February the Saudi and the Kuwaiti foreign ministers flew to Damascus to meet President Hafez al-Assad and his Iranian friends to warn them against invading Kuwait. They added that if he failed to restrain Iran he would lose subsidies from the Gulf states. As a result of this battle, Kuwait and – to a lesser degree – Saudi Arabia were under direct threat from Iran as Tehran was quick to remind them, yet paradoxically, Tehran's relations with the West and the Soviet Union improved and on 10 March a planned demonstration outside the Kuwaiti and Saudi embassies was hastily cancelled by the authorities, and when the protestors went ahead the demonstration was broken up by police.[31]

The outbreak of the Iran-Iraq War had made Kuwait and the other small Gulf oil producers acutely aware of their vulnerability,

and in May 1981 Bahrain, Kuwait, Oman, Qatar, Saudi Arabia, and the UAE created the Gulf Cooperation Council (GCC). They pledged to co-operate in a number of fields including defence, but the organisation stopped short of being a full alliance.[32] In September and October 1980 the Kuwaiti forces were placed on full alert with a military screen established along the border. Brigadier Muhammed Al-Bader became head of Operations and a joint command centre was created together with three plans. One was to defend the northern islands with 12 small strongpoints from Sabriya to the main offshore island, Bubiyan, manned by an infantry battalion of 6th Mechanised Brigade. The other two were based on a worse-case scenario in which the Iranians broke through to Basra and sought to invade Kuwait.

When the Iraqis requested a bridgehead in Kuwaiti territory, to thwart an Iranian attack, the battalion on Bubiyan Island was reinforced by a Chieftain MBT company.[33] To further thwart foreign interference, minefields were laid along the coast and a commando unit brought up as a tactical reserve. The air defences were supported by a Decca AR-1 air surveillance/air traffic control radar, a HAWK system and 'Grail' launchers. The country's air defences, however, depended upon a manually-operated sector operations centre pending the arrival of a Thomson-CSF computerised system. The Kuwaiti Air Force (Al-Quwwat al-Jawwiya al-Kuaitiya) was a small, still poorly-equipped force undergoing expansion: its dozen English Electric Lightning F.Mk 53s were meanwhile replaced by 27 Mirage F.1CK interceptors and six Mirage F.1BK trainers, while 36 Douglas A-4KU Skyhawk light attack aircraft were augmented by a dozen BAC Strikemaster T.Mk 83s. They proved inadequate in a few little-known clashes the IRIAF between 1981 and 1983 and incapable of disputing the IrAF use of Kuwaiti air space when its strike aircraft hunted shipping off the Iranian coast during the Tanker War. The rotary wing element consisted of eight Agusta-Bell 205s, two Bell 206s and 24 SA.342K Gazelles, while there were also two Lockheed C-130 Hercules transports.[34]

Attacks by pro-Iranian terrorists from mid-1983 saw the Kuwaiti armed forces also charged with internal defence plans. The first, 'al-Jeran' (The Neighbours) was to protect Kuwait City and the northern borders, while 'an-Nusar' (The Supporters) covered threats from the south with 80th (Internal Security) Brigade – formed under the Interior Ministry – to defend key sites. Relations with Iraq, which claimed Kuwait was a province, remained tense as the Kuwaitis wished to retain good relations with their powerful northern neighbour without surrendering their independence. They politely declined any Iraqi attempt in 1983 to lease Bubiyan Island – which became a military zone from which civilians were banned. They supported Baghdad's operations clandestinely, provided financial support and allowed convoys of up to 200 trucks at a time to drive northwards twice a week with Military Police escort.

With the nightmare scenario of an Iranian presence close to their borders and shells landing on Bubiyan Island, the Kuwaitis moved the 6th Brigade north in an arc to protect the approaches from Basra and the Faw Peninsula. Four offshore platforms with Rasit radars and electro-optical sensors were established by the Interior Ministry to prevent infiltration. The Kuwaitis were strongly supported by the Saudis who, in late March, declared that an attack upon Kuwait would be 'considered an attack on Saudi Arabia' and would result in full military assistance using the GCC Peninsular Shield force which was on stand-by at Hafra El Baten in Saudi Arabia. In August 1986, Iranian threats to launch surface-to-surface missiles at Kuwait if it continued its open support for Iraq led to Saudi troops being put on stand-by for possible deployment into Kuwait. In June, pro-Iranian Islamic fundamentalists were believed to have been responsible for bombs at oil export facilities which caused major fires in pipeline complexes and led Saddam to warn he would not tolerate Iranian-backed destabilisation of Kuwait and would be prepared to send in troops, which the Saudis opposed for fear it would be a tacit occupation.

Baghdad's dilemma

The Iraqis only gradually recognised that the enemy had opened a new front on the peninsula and awaited a major blow north of the Shatt until a captured IRIAF pilot revealed this was the prime operation.[35] Iraqi losses had been heavy, and while some estimates put them to 16 February at 5,000 and Iranian losses at 8,000-10,000, a more probable figure is 7,000 for the Iraqis and 8,000 for the Iranians (who admitted 800 dead), while the Iraqis had lost 20-25 aircraft.[36] The Iraqis lost three field batteries of 122mm and 130mm guns and up to 60 anti-aircraft guns of various calibres, as well as 1,500 prisoners. The blow to Saddam's prestige, and the corresponding increase in Iranian prestige, as well as diplomatic pressure from Saudi Arabia and his friends in the Gulf dictated his decision to regain the lost ground. But the profligate expenditure of artillery ammunition forced Baghdad to make emergency deals with individuals and manufacturers all over the world, no doubt at exorbitant financial cost.

The GMID assessed enemy strength in the south of the peninsula as 21st IRIA Division with four or five Pasdaran divisions; although the IRIA division was shortly transferred back across the Shatt and there were actually eight divisions and the equivalent of a ninth in the southern tip. To meet the immediate threat Rashid's III Corps lost a significant portion of its strength; 6th Armoured Division had already been committed, but would soon be returned to corps reserve, and was now joined by 5th Mechanised Division. IV Corps was ordered to despatch the Guards Division headquarters, together with 14th Infantry Division and 66th Commando Brigade, the armour coming south by rail.[37] Saddam appears to have visited the front on 12 February and recognised the need for a new front, as with the Marsh battles of 1984-1985, so Defence Minister Khairallah set up a forward General Headquarters at ad-Drehmiya camp 25 kilometres southwest of Basra, with the Chief of Staff and senior officers to co-ordinate a counter-offensive after personal battlefield tours.

This would be executed by three tactical headquarters or columns established on 13 February; the Northern Column (ar-Ratl ash-Shamaly) along the coastal highway was under Operations chief Lieutenant General Fakhri and based upon the Guards Armoured Division; the Central Column (ar-Ratl al-Wasaty) was under Major General Maher Abdul Rashid and would drive down the middle road spearheaded by 5th Mechanised Division (15th and 20th Mechanised Brigades) reinforcing the survivors of 26th Division; while the Southern Column (ar-Ratl al-Janoobi) under Major General Talia ad-Duri was around the axis of the Umm Qasr-Faw City road initially with the 440th and 441st Naval Brigades which were soon placed under the newly arrived 14th Infantry Division. Supporting them were three special forces and four commando brigades, and 15 artillery regiments which, along with divisional artillery, gave the Iraqis some 600 tubes together with MRLS and a 'Scud' regiment.

The counter-offensive began on 14 February, preceded by a major IrAF effort to knock out radars and air bases before the IrAF and IrAAC bombarded the bridgehead, which was also struck by 9K57 Luna (ASCC/NATO-code 'FROG-7') artillery rockets.[38] The effort was countered by the fact that the Iranians had brought up two I-HAWK launchers to cover the bridgeheads: these inflicted losses to Iraqi fighter-bombers and forced the IrAF to operate in much more elaborate strike packages. Still, Iranian death rates from air attacks using conventional and chemical weapons in the bridgeheads were estimated at one man per enemy sortie. Chemical weapons were used extensively and frequently proved effective because, although the Koran makes no mention of beards, the tradition was that The Prophet Mohammed had advocated Muslims to grow beards. This led to the practice (sunnah) of beards or at least trimmed moustaches which made it difficult to put on gas masks or to seal them.[39] The effects of chemical weapons were neutralised by the humid conditions and rain, although during February the Iranians reported 45,000 chemical casualties both here and on the northern battlefields and at least 100 were sent for treatment in Europe.

While the Iraqis had eight or nine brigades for the initial attack, the terrain severely limited their deployment to, essentially, a one-brigade front of around 5 kilometres, usually using an armoured or mechanised unit. It rained on most days between 14-18 February and with the ground already largely marsh the battlefield soon turned to churned up mud reminiscent of Third Ypres in 1917, indeed both sides probably suffered badly from Trench Foot. The coastal strip with its fields and palm groves allowed Fakhri to strike on a two-brigade front with a degree of cover, and artillery augmented by Astros MRLS which were especially effective against area targets. The defenders, however, could exploit former Iraqi strongpoints, fields, irrigation ditches and multiple berms.

Fakhri's attack proved a bloody disaster, with his troops coming under intense artillery fire, much of it across the Shatt, and attacks from Cobra gunships. They were quickly stopped and the follow-up forces piled up behind them to provide targets for Iranian gunners and airmen which meant they were only able to inch forward. By early afternoon they had stopped to lick their wounds and to build a new route to facilitate logistics. An Iraqi engineer officer remembered climbing onto an armoured engineer vehicle during the battle and said that while talking to the driver he was shaking with fear. His commander ordered a retreat. "I had to take it on the only paved road which was very dangerous because it was continuously being shelled and it was heavy, weighing more than 35 tonnes." There was a mortar battery and he watched as one tube after another was hit. An attack by the Southern Column also suffered heavy losses, partly due to IRIAF attacks, although Iraqi warships tried to interdict the coastal road.[40]

In a co-ordinated attack on 16 February, Guards Armoured Division had greater success, with artillery fire allowing the mechanised forces to approach within 400 metres of berms, which the IFVs and APCs would try to drive over although this exposed them to RPG fire. In a series of grim and bloody assaults the Iraqis managed to advance 2 kilometres before exhaustion brought them to a halt. Rashid's Central Column encountered well-dispersed Pasdarans with anti-armour missile launchers every 300 metres augmented by mobile 'Zolfaghar' anti-armour teams. From 18 February, these would receive some 500 American BGM-71 TOW missiles which had arrived at Bandar Abbas, followed by another 500 nine days later, most of which were expended against the Central Column. Unsurprisingly, the same managed to advance for exactly 600 metres.

The Iraqi counter-offensive

On the night of 16 to 17 February the Iranians began a major reinforcement effort while evacuating the wounded and improving defences by inundating land using water from the Shatt and the Khur Abdullah. The refreshed Iranians counter-attacked Rashid on the night of 17 to 18 February but were held, although this attack helped to slow the Iraqis whose progress over the next few days was the result of a host of carefully-planned small unit actions. On 18 February Iraq reported that Fakhri had been given command of the Faw sector and been replaced by General Saad Tumma al-Jubari.

By 19 February the Iraqi attack had to be abandoned in the face of heavy rain, hail and strong winds after an advance of 5.5 kilometres (3 kilometres by the Southern Column). Both sides recognised they were in an impasse; the Iraqis recognised they would not regain the Faw Peninsula and they began to fortify the southern approaches to Basra with berms stretching for kilometres, while at Friday prayers two days later Speaker Rafsanjani had to admit the Iranians had been forced to reduce their objectives merely to holding the peninsula.

The failure to retake the territory was a profound disappointment to Saddam, leading foreign observers to wonder whether or not it was due to a shortage of trained infantry. Some felt that 100,000 men would be needed to retake the Peninsula, rather than the 50,000 actually deployed. In the aftermath of the campaign they reported he had ordered reforms in training programmes, with dedicated combat training brigades emphasising the training of men to operate in all weather conditions.[41] Such reports may be exaggerated, but the Iraqis reduced the impact of the bitter fighting by exploiting the terrain limitations which limited the deployment of their divisions to brigades in echelon. Like Pétain at Verdun in 1916, the Iraqis rapidly rotated units, with 126 rotations during the campaign, which meant each brigade was in the line for only four or five days.

Yet they still suffered heavy casualties and special trains were organised to evacuate the wounded. There were enforced blood donations, attempts were made to recruit the staffs of leading tourist hotels wholesale, while taxis travelling north from Basrah had to carry corpses inside the vehicle and on roof-racks. The consumption of Iraqi war material was prodigious, up to 600 rounds per gun, and because tanks were used for infantry support it is reported that 200 worn-out tank gun barrels had to be replaced.[42] The Iraqis were placing great emphasis upon their artillery but shells tended to bury themselves before detonating, reducing their lethality and it probably led to greater emphasis upon air bursts. Much ammunition was wasted in random or area fire and Iraq desperately searched for replacement shells. The Iranians had their own problems and were finding it difficult to supply the two bridgeheads which may have had up to 70,000 troops between them.

On 20 February, Saddam again returned to the front to assess progress, as the IRIAF completed a series of strikes on forward Iraqi HQs and supply depots, enticing the Iraqis into several air battles east of the Faw Peninsula. Baghdad subsequently boasted about a loss of 45-47 fighters and 10 helicopters, crediting most of these to the Iranian air defences. However, to the present day there is only evidence for about a dozen losses in fighter bombers, and a similar number of helicopters. Even so, this cost the IrAF several highly experienced pilots and demoralized the reminder: Saddam's standing order for the air force to avoid losses was still in power and most of the air strikes were flown from medium altitude, which greatly diminished their precision. Saddam also ordered the IrAF into another round of air strikes on Iranian urban centres behind the frontline, and into additional attacks on the shipping around Khark Island, thus dissipating instead of concentrating the effort – while opening the skies for the Iranian transport helicopters, which – along with boats – continued bringing supplies and evacuating the wounded. Much more effective was the interdiction campaign ordered by the commander of the IrAF, Major-General Hamid Sha'aban. Ultimately, the IrAF flew 18,648 sorties over the Faw Peninsula between 9 February and 31 March (3,000 of these during the first week of the battle), averaging 365 a day.[43]

When Saddam finally granted them permission to run operations at their own discretion, Sha'ban ordered the IrAF to start flying at low altitudes again in order to improve precision of its air strikes: henceforth most fighter-bomber types did so – with the exception of those flying electronic-support missions, and Tu-16 and Tu-22 bombers. Flying low exposed the Iraqis to the full spectrum of Iranian air defences and caused several painful losses – even more so as next to no Iraqi aircrews that bailed out over the bridgeheads survived: furious ground troops tended to spray them with small-arms fire as they descended. The Iranians were aided by covert American supplies of I-HAWK missiles that greatly bolstered the half SAM-site that covered the peninsula, but also with spares for aircraft and missiles, augmented by spares from Israel, and it has been reported that the Iranians flew more than 1,000 sorties during the first fortnight. Up to 54 Iraqi aircraft and 20 helicopters were claimed as shot down in the Faw campaign, 20 of which were in the first week. Whatever their actual loss might have been, the Iraqis were meanwhile desperate enough to attempt cutting enemy pontoon bridges with the help of French-made AM.39 Exocet anti-ship missiles deployed from Aerospatiale SA.321 Super Frelon helicopters (one of which was shot down by Iranian fighters), while the Iraqi Navy was also called in to use its Osa-class fast attack craft and their P-15 (ASCC/NATO-code 'SS-N-2 Styx') missiles and claimed 'two supply vessels' as destroyed on 20 February.[44]

Saddam wanted to reduce Iraqi casualties retaking the Faw peninsula by ordering the avoidance of close quarter combat, and he also ordered III Corps commander Rashid to halt his advance. Rashid was a Takriti whose daughter was married to Saddam's youngest son. There was now an open confrontation between the two, although Rashid was a bit of a glory hound who boasted of stopping the Iranian 1984 offensive. He publicly confirmed the Iraqis had suffered heavy losses and reportedly blamed Saddam for ordering him to halt. Saddam recalled him to Baghdad and re-assigned him a northern corps.[45]

Saddam calls a halt

Fakhri appears to have recognised that his troops could do no more, but Saddam was in no mood to listen and demanded a renewed effort to retake the lost ground using leaders who had proven records of defeating the enemy attacks. Following another visit from Saddam on 23 February, General Sa'adi became VII Corps commander, while III Corps commander Rashid – who later told journalists Saddam had rejected his idea for counter-offensive across the river into Iranian territory – was given overall command of the counter-offensive. Finally, Fakhri took over the Central and Southern Columns which would now form the prime axis for regaining the peninsula. There was some re-organisation of the counter-attack forces and while the Northern Column was still autonomous under the Guards Division it began to integrate 19th Infantry Division, whose brigades edged their way towards the northeastern edge of the Mamlaha salt beds, with a view to replacing it. Meanwhile, poor weather, which lasted until 22 February, gave the Iranians a week to build up supplies and bring in reinforcements.[46]

The Iraqis renewed their counterattack on the night of 23 to 24

February, with Saddam in the command centre, but by now the Iranians had finally managed to bring in a number of batteries, for the first time on the peninsula there were major artillery duels. Rashid's force alone had 100 guns and fire direction observers operating from Pilatus PC-7 spotter aircraft transferred from Helicopter Combat Patrols, but here, as elsewhere along the front, the Iraqis preferred to saturate pre-selected artillery killing zones, indeed, for the first time they relied more on MRLS attacks rather than artillery fire to saturate areas with considerable success. These bombardments could be extremely destructive, although the Iranians had learned to disperse their forces while their counter-battery fire frequently forced the enemy batteries to move their guns.

Even with artillery and helicopter support the advance down the coastal highway was quickly brought to a halt, as the Pasdaran made repeated counter-attacks, usually at night in a vain attempt to avoid enemy artillery.[47] The Republican Guards received only limited armoured support and had to fight as conventional infantry, but in this sort of battle they lost their edge and had little hope of success. Eventually, the Guard retreated behind a barrage of high explosive and chemical shells – despite Baghdad's claims about driving a salient 1.35 kilometres long and 1 kilometre deep into the enemy positions.

The Republican Guard attacks

The battle continued raging to the south around the Mamlaha salt beds, already saturated with rain and which the defenders had flooded, turning them into marshes to confine Iraqi armour to the bunds and rendering them unable to manoeuvre the Iranians out of their positions. With their attacks channelled into narrow fronts where there was fierce fighting, the Iraqis were vulnerable to anti-armour missiles, especially TOW with its range of 3.75 kilometres. The offensive petered out after a few days. The Central Column made the greatest progress advancing 1.6 kilometres deep and 2 kilometres wide on 23 February, despite a setback caused by the Iranian COMINT: as a staff meeting was held at the forward command post of the 5th Mechanised Division, this was precisely shelled and numerous officers hit. The dead included divisional commander General Hayyan and several staff officers. This failure temporarily halted its progress once it had taken the 'third embankment' in the salt beds.[48] Despite this, the column advanced a further 2.5 kilometres the next day, while on the night of 26 to 27 February the Northern Column's 19th Infantry Division's attack gained sufficient ground to expose Iranian positions and compel them to move. The campaign now ground to a halt, although the Iraqi Navy claimed success on 26 February in destroying a bridge which the enemy were building between Abadan and al-Bisha Cape. The following day Saddam returned to Baghdad but he had left orders that the campaign was to continue even though it had reportedly cost the Iraqis some 10,000 casualties.

The Central Column with 19th Division inched forward, while the Southern Column took the western section of the salt beds provoking the Pasdaran to make three nights of mass attacks to regain the lost ground. They suffered from the same tactical conditions as the Iraqis however, and their waves of troops dissolved under heavy artillery fire. Further counter-attacks were launched along the whole front on the night of 2 to 3 March resulting in heavy fighting which lasted seven hours, with Iraqi artillery turning night into day. Another attack was beaten off on the night of 11 to 12 March as Rashid slowly advanced, but co-ordination between the columns sometimes failed and on one occasion the Central and Southern Columns exchanged fire. The battle was rapidly approaching an impasse and an attempt by naval and heliborne commandos on the night of 9 to 10 March was eventually repulsed because the Pasdaran had dispersed and camouflaged their forces.

The front is closed down

On 12 March the Defence Minister and Chief of Staff visited the front to assess the situation after 6th Armoured Division failed to draw away reserves following a dummy attempt to cross the Shatt on 7 March. The Iraqi leaders still hoped it might be possible to recapture the whole peninsula but despite knowing that their fire was causing the enemy heavy losses, as confirmed by COMINT which intercepted pleas for help to evacuate the wounded, Iranian resistance continued and progress had slowed. Although the Northern Column conducted raids on the enemy during the night from 23 to 24 March, by 21 March all Iraqi progress had ceased and they could only interdict enemy supply lines, including launching 250 FROG-7 missiles as well as chemical weapons. As the weather improved in late March, the IrAF joined in, but the Iraqis were now concentrating upon building defences.

Between 31 March and 1 April Saddam presided two conferences at the GHQ, the first lasting 9 and the second 11 hours. Both were 'post mortem' and merely resulted in a re-consideration of the future policy. The Iraqi Army clearly had major problems and thus it was decided to rubber stamp a decision made ten days earlier to alter the way of fighting. With the Iranians driven close to the salt pans, the offensives which were simply causing casualties were now to be stopped and the defences strengthened. The road system was also to be improved while the chance was taken to pull out some of VII Corps' units from the line for re-organisation and training. The corps was reinforced by the 37th and 42nd Infantry Divisions, both led by officers who had distinguished themselves in the fighting. Under such circumstances, the fighting along the frontlines deteriorated into low-level clashes and bombardment: indeed, after the last minor Iraqi attack on 20 September, both sides settled down.

By then the Iraqis were running a massive engineering work, building defensive systems for a later attack including positions for armoured vehicles, artillery and mortars, as well as helicopter landing pads. Civilian ministries were called in to assist with this work and helped to build 1,100 kilometres of road, 1,060 kilometres of defensive works, 16 kilometres of canals and 16 bridges. The General Staff Planning and Operations Departments beginning examining for, and preparing, plans to recapture the peninsula; with 14 working meetings from 14 May 1986 when the order was given to begin the work. On 16 June a joint service planning group under the Army Minister General Abdul Jabbar Henschel was established which was later joined by VII Corps chief of staff.[49]

The victory boosted Iranian self confidence and Khomeini issued a fatwa demanding the war be ended by the next Iranian new year (March 1987), but Tehran also continued to reject diplomatic efforts to end the conflict. Valfajr-8 left the Iranians holding more enemy territory following a brilliant start, but it was strategically almost useless and they were certainly no nearer Basra. As one of their soldiers later said:

'We were full of confidence and were waiting for orders to march to Basrah. Instead, to our great disappointment, we were told to stay put.'[50]

In exchange for 20,000-30,000 casualties (including 400 prisoners) Tehran had taken a bridgehead some 16 kilometres north of al-Faw, they claimed to have destroyed 500 armoured vehicles and 35 artillery pieces. During the summer most of the assault divisions were withdrawn from the peninsula and sent to the assembly camps between Ahwaz and Khorammshahr and were mostly replaced by Pasdaran naval brigades, while some Pasdaran 'Silkworms' were moved into the abandoned al-Bisha Cape missile launching facilities to threaten Kuwaiti oil loading.

Conclusions

Valfajr-8 demonstrated that Iran could achieve strategic surprise even in the face of US satellite technology and major Iraqi advances in the field of COMINT/SIGINT, and that the Iranian commanders were now capable of running coordinated multi-corps offensives on several fronts. Their troops had demonstrated their ability to fight a successful defence in depth, too. One commentator pointed out:

'Valfajr-8 constituted the high point of Iran's war effort and has generally been hailed as its most successful operation. It rekindled the hopes of Iran's leadership — falsely, as it would turn out — that Saddam Hussein's regime was on the verge of collapse.... Although they had failed to completely cut the Iraqis off from the sea (the latter retained a very narrow foot-hold on the Gulf through Umm Qasr), the Iranians' capture and retention of Faw was a major blow to Saddam's prestige'.[51]

Yet ultimately, 'Valfajr' was an attempt to demonstrate the much quoted claim that 'war is an extension of diplomacy through other means' attributed to military philosopher Carl von Clausewitz. Although often described as an attempt to envelop Basra from the south, the offensive was really Tehran's attempt to break the 'oil conspiracy'. Had it been a serious attempt to threaten Basra then the main force would have been deployed in the northern bridgehead not the southern one. Here it was impossible to exploit the tactical success with rapid and substantial reinforcements of vehicles, without which the Iranians faced a week-long march on foot to reach Basra. This was clearly impossible in the face of superior Iraqi firepower and transport capacities, and the only conclusion left was that the main blow was in the south purely to threaten Kuwait through a significant Iranian presence on the al-Faw Peninsula. But far from cowing the Kuwaitis and Saudis it frightened them into giving Saddam greater financial and diplomatic support as their shield against the Iranians. The Arab League committee (Iraq, Saudi Arabia, Kuwait, Yemen, Jordan, Tunisia and Morocco) met hurriedly in Baghdad on 12 February and denounced Iran's 'intransigent attitude', warning that the new offensive could seriously damage Arab-Iranian relations.[52]

Tactically, it was clear that the Iranians still had much to learn with regards to logistics, for their failure to exploit the initial success was due to their inability to maintain a steady flow of supplies necessary for sustaining an advance. There were some grounds for optimism, for during the course of operations Iranian commanders demonstrated a degree of flexibility, diverting troops and resources from one sector to another when they achieved a breakthrough, in order to reinforce success. Yet ultimately, it reflected Tehran's chronic shortage of armour and artillery as well as the men who could best exploit them. With nothing more to achieve, Tehran reduced the garrison on the peninsula withdrawing the regular units and leaving the equivalent of two Pasdaran divisions, but IRIA engineers, with their Pasdaran and civilian comrades provided them with numerous berms, improved communications and flooded areas to impede enemy movement. Moreover, another five divisions (85,000 men) remained in the Khorramshahr/Abadan area to threaten the Iraqis.[53]

Iraqi casualties were up to 12,000 (including 2,100 prisoners) many of whom were veteran troops and airmen. The Republican Guards lost a third of the men deployed in a bitter battle of attrition. The Iraqis were caught wrong-footed and while they were able to slam the door to contain the threat, the terrain and weather prevented them eliminating it as their leaders undoubtedly hoped. Yet the extent of Saddam Hussein's resolve to retake the Faw Peninsula can be gauged by the number of Iraqi air sorties flown: 18,548 between 9 February and 25 March, compared to 20,011 for all of 1985.[54]

The loss of territory finally convinced Saddam Hussein from July to allow the generals greater initiative possibly to distance himself and the Ba'ath from any disasters which might occur. Although Iraq's total manpower losses were probably half those of Iran, this ratio was unacceptable to Baghdad, partly because its losses included many skilled pilots and technicians who could not be easily replaced, and partly because of the demographic imbalance between the two countries.

The staff received permission to convert the Republican Guard into a military shock force with the Republican Guards Command initially allocated six brigades, only to be tripled in size during the next year, while early in 1987 three divisions were created under the Republican Guard Ground Forces Command. Its troops, and those of the best army units, i.e. the 3rd, 6th and 10th Armoured Divisions with 1st and 5th Mechanised Divisions, were given extensive training in combined-arms operations and offensive tactics. They practised constantly and conducted manoeuvres in corps strength as well as receiving the latest equipment such as T-72 tanks, BMP-1 infantry combat vehicles, GCT self-propelled artillery, and GHN-45 and G-5 towed artillery. Stripping the remainder of the army weakened much of it, but the 11 divisions ultimately available, including Special Forces and Guards, provided an offensive capability described as 'modest' by one commentator who certainly under-estimated it.[55] Strategically the idea was sown that Iraq could not achieve victory while remaining upon the defensive and that at some time it would have to resume its own major offensives.

The Iraqi general staff were not optimistic about the capabilities of the new force. Recognising that its leaders did not possess the personal initiative to conduct operations, the Deputy Chief of Staff (Operations), General Hussein Rashid Muhammad at-Tikriti directed the creation of detailed and innovative scripts for every conceivable offensive and counter-offensive operation. The commanders then received the scripts which they would learn by heart and practise for months, often over full-size mock-ups of the terrain in which these operations were to be executed. The units would continually rehearse their missions with units repeating specific tasks until they were word perfect, then these would be repeatedly practised by the units individually, then collectively, so the operation could be performed from memory.[56] The professionalism of the Iraqi armed forces also extended into the air force, which was now under the new, aggressive, commander Major General Hamid Shabban, was allowed to increase the number of sorties per mission and accept the heavier loss rates in return for improved performance.

With the conclusion of the Faw campaign, fighting for almost all of 1986 was confined to the central and northern fronts. There were continued raids and during one, Iran's Operation 'Karbala 3' on 1 and 2 September, they took the oil terminal and its radar set at al-Ummaya. Yet the Iranians were simply biding their time before renewing their assault upon Basra. It took nine months to prepare for this, but on 24 December they launched Operation 'Karbala 4', which proved an unmitigated disaster, but was soon followed by 'Karbala 5' which would prove a decisive blow, but not in the way Tehran had anticipated.

Bibliography

BOOKS

Buchan, James. *Days of God: The Revolution in Iran and its Consequences* (London: John Murray, 2013)

Cooper, Tom & Bishop, Farzad. *Iran-Iraq War in the Air 1980-1988.* (Atglen: Schiffer Military History, 2000)

Cooper, T., & Sipos, M., *Iraqi Mirages: The Dassault Mirage Family in Service with the Iraqi Air Force, 1981-1988* (Warwick, Helion & Co., 2019; ISBN 978-1-912390-31-1)

Cordsman, Anthony H. *The Iran-Iraq War and Western Security 1984-1987.* (London: Jane's Publishing Company Ltd, 1987)

Cordsman, Anthony H. & Wagner, Abraham R. *The Lessons of Modern War: Volume II - The Iran-Iraq War* (Boulder/San Francisco: Westview Press, 1990/London: Mansell Publishing Ltd, 1990)

Dunston, Simon. *Chieftain Main Battle Tank 1965-2003* (Oxford: Osprey Publishing, 2003)

Farouk, Dr Kaveh. *Iran at War 1500-1980* (Botley: Osprey Publishing, 2011)

Foss, Christopher. *Jane's Armour and Artillery, 1980-2007* (Coulsdon: Jane's Information Group, 1980-2007).

Hiro, Dilip. *The Longest War: The Iran-Iraq Military Conflict* (London: Paladin Grafton Books, 1989)

International Institute for Strategic Studies. *The Military Balance 1980-1982* (London: 1980-1982)

De Lestapis, Jacques (Ed). *Military Powers Encyclopedia, League of Arab States; Irak, Jordan, Lebanon, Syria, PLO, Iran, Israel* (Paris: Society I³C, 1989)

Malovany, Lieutenant Colonel Pesach. *Milhamot Bavel ha-Hadasha (The Wars of Modern Babylon)* (Tel Aviv: Malarakhot, 2010)

Al-Marashi, Ibrahim & Salama, Sammy. *Iraq's Armed Forces: An analytical history* (London: Routledge, 2009)

Murray, Williamson & Woods, Kevin M. *The Iran-Iraq War: A Military and Strategic History* (Cambridge: Cambridge University Press, 2014)

National Training Center. *The Iraqi Army: Organization and Tactics* (Colorado: Paladin Press, Boulder, 1991)

Nejad, Parviz Mosalla (Editor). *Shalamcheh* (Shalamcheh: Sarir Publication, 2006)

Downloaded from web site Shalamcheh Author: The Hub of Resistance Literature & History (http)sajed.ir/upload%5Ctopic%5Cebook-Shalamcheh.pdf

O'Ballance, Edgar. *The Gulf War* (London: Brassey's Defence Publishers, 1988)

Pelletiere, Stephen C. *The Iran-Iraq War: Chaos in a Vacuum* (Westport CT and London: Praeger, 1992)

Pollack, Kenneth M. *Arabs at War. Military Effectiveness 1948-1991* (Lincoln & London: University of Nebraska Press, 2002)

Pollack, Kenneth. *The Persian Puzzle* (New York: Random House, 2004)

Rottman, Gordon L. *The Rocket Propelled Grenade* (Botley: Osprey Publishing, 2010)

Schmidt, Rachel. *Global Arms Exports to Iraq, 1960-1990* (Santa Monica: California, RAND, 1991)

Stockholm International Peace Research Institute (SIPRI). *Yearbooks 1980-1989. World Armaments and Disarmament* (Oxford: University Press, 1980-1989)

Ward, Steven R. *Immortal: A Military History of Iran and its Armed Forces* (Washington DC: Georgetown University Press, 2009)

Woods, Kevin M. (With Williamson Murray & Thomas Holaday with Mounir Elkhamri). *Saddam's War: An Iraqi Military Perspective of The Iran-Iraq War* (Washington DC: United States Dept. of Defence (McNair Papers), 2009)

Woods, Kevin M. (With Williamson Murray & Thomas Holaday with Mounir Elkhamri). *Project 1946* (Alexandria: Virginia, Institute for Defense Analyses, 2008)

Woods, Kevin M. (With Murray Williamson, Elizabeth A. Nathan, Laila Sabara, Ana M.Veneger). *Saddam's Generals: Perspectives of the Iran-Iraq War* (Alexandria, Va: Institute for Defense Analysis, 2010) US Arms Control and Disarmament Agency. *World Military Expenditures and Arms Transfers 1972-1982* (Washington DC: 1984)

Zabih, Sepehr. *The Iranian Military in Revolution and War* (London: Routledge, 1988) New version published 2011 as part of Routledge Library Editions: Iran, Routledge, Abingdon, 2011 ISBN 978-0-415-57033-6. Author as Sepehr Zabir

ARTICLES, ESSAYS, MONOGRAPHS, PAPERS, THESES

Abramowitz, Jeff, Jacqueline Hahn, Jerry Cheslow. *Iraq: the military build-up* (IDF Journal, Volume III, No 2., Spring 1986)

Atkeson, Major General Edward B. *Iraq's Arsenal: Tool of Ambition* (Army, March 1991 pp. 22-30)

Beuttel, H.W. *Iranian casualties in the Iran-Iraq War: A re-appraisal Parts 1 & 2* (TNDM, Vol 2, No 3., December 1997 and Vol 2, No 4., December 1998)

Cooper, Tom and Bishop, Farzad. *Fire in the Hills: Iraq and Iran in Conflict* (Air Enthusiast Issue 104, March/April 2003. pp.14-24)

Davis, Major Mark J. *Iranians' Operational Warfighting Ability: An Historical Assessment and View to the Future* (School of Advanced Military Studies, United States Army and Command General Staff College, Fort Leavenworth, Kansas, 1992)

Griffin, Lieutenant Colonel Gary B. *The Iraqi Way of War: An Operational Assessment* (School of Advanced Military Studies, United States Army Command and General Staff College, Fort Leavenworth, Kansas, 1990)

No author. *The international arms industry: Final casualty of the Gulf War,* (Jane's Defence Weekly, July 30 1988.)

O'Ballance, Colonel Edgar. *Iran vs Iraq: Quantity vs Quality?* (Defence Attache No 1/1987 pp.25-31)

Samuel, Annie Tracy. *Perceptions and Narratives of Security: The Iranian Revolutionary Guards Corps and the Iran-Iraq War. Discussion Paper 2012-06* (Belfer Center for Science and International Affairs, John F.Kennedy School of Government, Harvard University, Cambridge, Mass 2012)

Tucker, A.R *Armored Warfare in the Gulf,* (Armed Forces, May 1988, pp.223-226)

Various periodicals published by the Iranian and Iraqi Ministries of Defence, 1980s, 1990s, and 2000s.

DOCUMENTS

Conflict Record Research Center (CRRC)

SH-GMID-D-000-531: General Military Intelligence Directorate (GMID) Intelligence Reports about Iranian Force Movements during the Iran-Iraq War. April-May 1982

SH-GMD-D-000-842: General Military Intelligence Directorate Report Assessing Political, Military and Economic Conditions in Iran. Probably July 1980.

SH-MISC-D-000-827: Saddam and Senior Iraqi Officials Discussing the Conflict with Iran, Iraqi Targets and Plans, a recent Attack on the Osirak Reactor, and Various Foreign Countries. October 1, 1980.

SH-MISC-D-001-350: The Passing of Two Years of War: Iran-Iraq, Political Office of the Islamic Revolution Pasdaran Corps.

SH-PDWN-D-001-021: Transcripts of Meetings Between Saddam and Senior Iraqi Officials Discussing Military Tactics During the War with Iran, Including the Use of Napalm and Cluster Bombs, Tank Maneuvering and Attacking Oil Refineries. Meeting on October 6 1980.

SP-PDWN-D-000-552: Documents from the Presidential Diwan regarding arms agreements signed between Iraq and the Soviet Union in 1981 and 1983.

SH–SHTP-A-000-835: Saddam and His Advisors Discussing Iraq's Decision to Go to War with Iran September 16, 1980.

SH-SHTP-D-000-856: Transcript of a Meeting between Saddam Hussein and the Armed Forces General Command. November 22, 1980.

Defense Intelligence Agency

DDB-1100-IZ-81: Ground Order of Battle-Iraq (March 1981)

DDB-1100-342-86: Ground Forces Intelligence Study-Iran (May 1986)

DDB-1100-343-85: Ground Forces Intelligence Study: Iraq (November 1985)

DDB-2680-103-88 Part II: Military Intelligence Summary: Volume III, Part II Middle East and North Africa (Persian Gulf) (Cut-off date 1 July 1987)

UK National Archives

BT 241/2929: Iran – Military Supplies

FCO 8/2793: Sale of Chieftain Tanks from the United Kingdom to Iraq 1976

FCO 8/2845: UK Defence Sales to Iraq

FCO8/ 3020: Report of Defence Attaché's, Baghdad September 1979

FCO 8/3023: Sale of Chieftain Tanks from UK to Iraq 1977

FCO 8/3124: Arms Sales to Iran 1978

FCO 8/3135: Sale of Shir Iran Main Battle Tanks to Iran

FCO 8/3624: Supply of Military Equipment to Iran

FCO 8/3715: Defence Attache's Annual Report on Iraq 1980

FCO 8/3841: Head of Defence Sales Visits to the Gulf.

FCO 8/4146: Defence Sales to Iraq: Tanks

FCO 8/4156: UK Defence Attache's Annual Report 1981

FCO 8/4162: Sale of Barmine and Ranger to Iraq

FCO 8/4164: Sale of Tanks to Iraq

WO341/204: Report on Shir I (FV 4030)

US Army Intelligence and Security Command

Untitled and undated history of Iran-Iraq War from September 1980 to the spring of 1983. Released under NGIA FOIA request NGA #20130255F and US Army Intelligence and Security Command request FOIA#2456F-12 on November 19, 2013. Declassified March 19, 2013.

Web sites

Ahwaz Climate, world-climates.com

Country Study and Country guide, Iran, allrefer.com

Cipher Machines website ciphermachines.com

Climatological Normals of Abadan hko.gov.hk

Freemeteo website, freemeteo.com.

Iranian Army, iiarmy.topcities.com

Imposed War web site, sajed.ir, English.tebyan,net, Ironsides8m.com/army/ir.htm~army

Weather History, Kuwait and Diyarkabir, harvardmun.org

Notes

Chapter 1

1 Based upon Michael Connell's study *Iranian Operational Decision Making*, pp.6-9 (hereafter 'Connell'); Dilip Hiro, *The Longest War*, pp.86-87 (hereafter 'Hiro'), and Edgar O'Ballance, *The Gulf War*, pp.95-96 (hereafter 'O'Ballance').

2 The Badr Brigades have continued to exist in one form or another as a Shi'a militia, even after Hakim was assassinated by a car bomb three months after returning to Iraq in 2003. At the time of writing, they are engaging the forces of the notorious terrorist movement 'Islamic State'.

3 Hiro, pp.86-87.

4 Woods et al, *Project 1946*, p.78 (hereafter '*Project 1946*'). The US Army Intelligence and Security Command History of the Iran-Iraq War from September 1980 to the Spring of 1983 (hereafter US AISC) gives the geographic co-ordinates as 30-52N/48-00E to 30-43N/47-47E. For the defences, see Buchan, *Days of God*, p.355 (hereafter Buchan); Cordesman et al, *The Lessons of Modern War Vol II*, p.149 (hereafter '*Lessons*'); Hiro, pp.180-181; Nejad, *Shalamcheh*, pp.24, 28-29 (hereafter 'Nejad'); Pollack, *Arabs at War*, pp.203-204 (hereafter 'Pollack'); US AISC, pp.6-15 & '*Abandoned fortifications of the Iran-Iraq War*', Virtualglobetrotting website.

5 For these defences, see National Training Center, *The Iraqi Army: Organization and Tactics*, pp.150, 153-154 (hereafter NTC).

6 Nejad, pp.22-23.

7 AISC, pp.6-15; Williamson Murray and Kevin M. Woods, *The Iran-Iraq War*, p.193 (hereafter Murray et al), claim 90,000. About a third of the Iranian troops were IRIA.

8 For Operation Ramadan al-Mubarak, see Connell, pp.10-21; Tom Cooper & Farzad Bishop, *Iran-Iraq War in the Air*, p.138 (hereafter Cooper & Bishop); Hiro, p.87; *Lessons*, pp.150-151; Kaveh Farrokh, *Iran at War*, pp.370-371 (hereafter Farrokh); Pesach Malovany, Milhamot Bavel ha-Hadasha (*The Wars of Modern Babylon*), pp.216-225 (hereafter Malovany); Murray & Woods, pp.192-196; Nejad, pp.22-29; O'Ballance, pp.93-98; Stephen C. Pelletiere, *The Iran-Iraq War*, pp.63-64 (hereafter Pelletiere); Pollack, pp.204-205; Steven R. Ward, *Immortal*, pp.259-260 (hereafter 'Ward'); Stepher Zabih, *The Iranian Military*, p.181 (hereafter 'Zabih'); AISC, pp.61-12, 6-15, 6-19, Fig. 6-10, 6-17. Even if frequently drawing wrong conclusions about the reasons, O'Ballance and Pollack have the most detailed accounts, while we would like to acknowledge our deep gratitude for assistance and advice of General Makki.

9 Cooper & Bishop, p.137. The Israelis supplied US$100 million worth of aircraft spares between May 1980 and June 1981, but curtailed supplies about the time the Iranian offensive began.

10 All weather data is based upon the Kuwait weather forecast, Weather History, daily archive in Freemeteo website, Kuwait archive for the period 1980-1988.

11 Sa'adi Tumma would become Deputy Chief of Staff for Training and Doctrine, in the spring of 1984.

12. Woods et al, *Saddam's Generals*, pp.124-125 (hereafter Woods, *Generals*). We are again very grateful to General Makki for additional background information.
13. Murray & Woods, p.185.
14. Pollack, p.208.
15. DIA Document DDB-1100-343-85, pp.61, 65-67.
16. Lessons, p.149; AISC, p.6-12. Murray & Woods (p.193) claim 70,000 men.
17. Buchan, p.352.
18. Farrokh, pp.368-369.
19. Iranian police had used tear gas during the defence of Khorramshahr, in October-November 1980.
20. N Rassi, a former Chieftain-tank commander, then company commander of the IRIA, interview, February 2003.
21. Simon Dunstan, *Chieftain Main Battle Tank*, p.6.
22. Adar Forouzan to Ed McCaul, Military History magazine, Vol.21/No.1 (Herndon, Va., April 2004), pp.44ff, in Buchan, pp.356-357.
23. Brigadier-General Sadik recalled that Khairallah once nearly caused a collision with one of the IrAF's fighter-bombers while 'touring' the battlefield near Basrah in one of the helicopters he flew on his own (Sadik, interview, March 2005).
24. For the air war, see Cooper & Bishop, and the same authors' article '*Fire in the Hills*' (hereafter 'Cooper & Bishop, *Hills*') and Cooper & Smisek, *Iraqi Mirages*.
25. Cooper & Bishop, p.133; Cooper & Bishiop, *Hills*, p.20; AISC, p.6-15. The obsolete Swatter used five VHF radio channels, but Spiral had a radio-command link guidance.
26. Tawfik was a Sandhurst graduate and was actually a year senior to Makki, who graduated from Sandhurst a year later. Before assuming command of 8th Infantry Division, he had been commandant of the Iraqi Military Collage. He would later be commander of II Corps for a while, before becoming the first President of the Military Academy (information from General Makki).
27. For the disbandment of the 9th Armoured Division and its aftermath, see Murray & Woods, p.63 & Woods, *Generals*, pp.16, 31-32, 39.
28. Higher casualties were estimated by Pelletiere at 27,000, and *Lessons*, at 20,000-30,000.
29. Ward, p.260.
30. Rassi noted he left the army after seeing a Pasadaran commander launching an attack before any artillery preparation, with the result that his troops were smashed by enemy artillery while approaching Iraqi positions (interview, February 2003).
31. Ward, p.260.
32. Farrokh, pp.367-368.
33. AISC, p.6-29.
34. Cooper & Bishop, p.138 & DIA DDB-110-343-85, p.50.
35. Cordesman, pp.442-444 & *Project 1946*, p.53.
36. Nejad, pp.28-29.
37. General Nizar Abdulkareem Faysal al-Khazraji, *al-Harb al-Iraqiya – al-Iraniya: Muthekerat Muqatel (Iran-Iraq War 1980-1988 – Memoirs of a Combatant)*, Beirut: Arab Centre for Research and Policies, date unclear, pp.281-282 – kindly forwarded by General Makki.

Chapter 2

1. *Jane's Defence Weekly*, March 24, 1984, Iran discusses war aims amid major new assaults.
2. These will be discussed in the Volume IV (detailing the northern and central Fronts); Pelletiere pp.79-80.
3. Anthony H. Cordesman, *The Iran-Iraq War*, p.61 (hereafter, Cordesman). After the war to drive out the pro-Shia inhabitants, the Iraqis drained a substantial portion of the marshes by diverting water, damming tributaries, and building embankments along the banks of the Tigris. By 2002, only a third remained, but with the fall of Saddam efforts are now being made to restore the marshes and turn them into a nature reserve.
4. After the war deeper drilling discovered further reserves and the new field was estimated to have 23-25 billion barrels and by the beginning of the 21st Century the state-owned Southern Oil Company was producing 50,000 barrels/day just from the developed part of the Majnoon field.
5. Other estimates put the number of production and exploration rigs in Majnoon at 52. The Nahr Umr field was discovered in 1949 and was estimated at 6 billion barrels of oil but had been regarded as too small to develop, but drilling by Petrobras showed the field was much larger than originally estimated.
6. Farrokh p.375 & Ward pp.259-260. Khyber is also written as Khaibar, Kheybar and Khybar – and was originally an oasis north of Medina through which the Prophet travelled before his return to Mecca.
7. The passages on the Pasdaran are based upon CRRC SH-GMID-D-000-529, and Iranian accounts of Khyber. Buchan p.351; Ward pp.246-247.
8. Married clerics appear to have brought their families to towns near their encampments.
9. For a study of the problem for Iranian troops during the war see Tavana's article on the disease during the war.
10. For the Basiji see Ward pp.246-247; Woods, Generals p.35; Edgar O'Ballance article *Iran vs Iraq*; DIA DDB-1100-342-86 p.46); for the rest, Zabih p.220. Pals Battalions were raised from men from local communities or in similar employment. The traditions of one such battalion, the Artists' Rifles, were retained to form the Special Air Service.
11. Cordesman p.63.
12. For Operation 'Khyber' see Buchan pp.359-360; Cooper & Bishop pp.165-168; Cordesman pp.61-63; Farrokh pp.377-379; Hiro pp.103-105; Lessons pp.179-183; Malovany pp.259-272; Ibrahim Al-Marashi & Sammy Salam, *Iraq's Armed Forces* p.158, hereafter Marashi & Salama; Murray & Woods pp.228-230; O'Ballance pp.143-148; Pelletiere pp.82, 87-92; Ward pp.264-265; Woods, Generals pp.126-128; Zabih pp.186-188. We would also like to express my particular thanks to General Makki for additional information.
13. DIA DDB-1100-342-86 p.25. Post-war Pasdaran accounts claim that the bridge itself was the final objective, which is inaccurate. Jalali was IRIAA commander from 25 June 1983 until 23 October 1985, and then became Defence Minister. After the war he would command the Pasdaran Air Force and later become a defence advisor.
14. O'Ballance p.144 & DIA DDB-1100-342-86, p.25.
15. CRRC SH-AFGC-D-000-686; Makki in Woods, *Generals* p.127 (however, on p.73 he was described as 'one of the dumbest generals in the army' by Republican Guard commander General Ra'ad al-Hamdani). Rashid was a Saddam loyalist who spent many years in jail in post-Saddam Iraq and died in 2014 near Tikrit.
16. The 426th Infantry Brigade took no part in the battle. For details, see SH-GMID-D-000-30 & Woods, *Project 1946*, p.78.
17. Woods, *Generals*, pp.126-127.
18. CRRC SH-AFGC-D-000-686 & Woods, *Project 1946*, p.94.
19. Cordesman p.62 & Lessons, p.181.
20. Hiro p.104.
21. Woods, *Generals* pp.126-127; CRRC SH-AFGC-D-000-686; DIA DDB-1100-343-85 p.13. The Iraqi name was Quiadet Amaliyat Sharq-Dijilah or 'East of Tigris Command' but ETOH will be used to avoid confusing the reader. Commando brigades (Alwiyat al-Maqhaweer), numbered from 60 upwards, were assault troop units used as reaction and sometimes as raiding forces. Special forces brigades (Alwiyat al-Quwat al-Khassah) were trained to operate behind enemy lines, although rarely did so.
22. Cooper & Bishop pp. 167-168.
23. *Sunday Times*, 18 March 1984; *Jane's Defence Quarterly*, 25 January 1984; Buchan (p.356) reported the conversation with Pasdaran veteran in 1999.
24. DIA DDB-1100-342-86 p.25.
25. Major Mark J. Davis, *Iranians' Operational Warfighting Ability*, p.11 (hereafter Davis) & DIA DDB-1100-342-86, p.42.